TRAVELER'S TRIVIA TEST

Revised

1,101 Questions and Answers for the Sophisticated Globetrotter

George Blagowidow

HIPPOCRENE BOOKS
New York

QUESTIONS...

1. In what city can you see the original statue of David by Michaelangelo?

2. Where does the Blue Nile meet the White Nile, creating a spectacular view?

3. In what Spanish town can you visit Salvador Dali's birthplace and a museum dedicated to his works?

4. In what town is Koenigsallee, a street planned by Napoleon, the main shopping center?

5. There are many beaches throughout the world covered with pebbles, but there is one famous beach in the U.S.A. actually called Pebble Beach. Where is it?

6. What do you call a popular establishment to have a drink and some food in France?

7. What famous Chinese city is known for the beauty of its stone gardens-a segment of one has been reconstructed in the Metropolitan Museum in New York?

8. Istanbul is a modern metropolis in Turkey. If you had visited it in ancient times what would it have been called?

9. Name the southernmost, the easternmost, the westernmost, and the northernmost states of the U.S.A.

10. In which country can you take a steam bath at the health resort that was the first to be called a "spa"?

...ANSWERS

1. Florence, Italy
2. Khartoum, Sudan
3. Figueras, Spain
4. Dusseldorf, Germany
5. Monterey peninsula, California
6. *Bistro*
7. Suzhou
8. Constantinople
9. Hawaii, Alaska, Alaska, Alaska
10. Belgium

QUESTIONS...

11. On what Mediterranean island is Costa Smeralda?

12. In which modern country can you see the ruins of Carthage?

13. The Polish currency *zloty* can be divided into 100 what?

14. Name the country that supplies most of the world's need for rose oil.

15. In what country is *goulash* served as the culinary specialty?

16. The Rubens house can be visited in the city of his birth. Name the city.

17. To see the panda in its natural habitat you must go to a single province of one country. Name them.

18. What internationally famous museum can be toured in Leningrad, U.S.S.R.?

19. What are Ely and Peterborough, both in England, famous for?

20. Where in the U.S.A. should you make reservations to dine in the oldest restaurant to operate continuously in the same building?

...ANSWERS

11. Sardinia, Italy
12. Tunisia
13. *Groszy*
14. Bulgaria
15. Hungary
16. Antwerp, Belgium
17. Szechwan, China
18. Hermitage
19. Cathedrals
20. King George Inn, Bristol, Pennsylvania

QUESTIONS...

21. In what city is it a tradition to throw coins in the fountain Trevi?

22. Which Caribbean islands are called the ABC islands?

23. Where can you safari through the largest natural wildlife preserve?

24. Sailing on what river will you pass 3 European capital cities? Name the cities too!

25. In what city can you visit the Wallace collection?

26. An aromatic honey is collected from a plant called wildwood. Name the only island on which it grows.

27. To what town in Portugal do millions of Catholics make a pilgrimage each year?

28. What U.S. city claims to be the "Pheasant World Capital"?

29. One of the fiercest battles of World War II was fought at Stalingrad. What was the former name of this city? What is it called today?

30. In what country can you see the vineyards which produce the wine *Rioja*?

21. Rome, Italy
22. Aruba, Bonaire, Curacao
23. Niger, Africa
24. Danube; Vienna, Budapest, Belgrade
25. London, England
26. Tasmania, Australia
27. Fatima
28. Huron, South Dakota
29. Carycyn; Volgograd
30. Spain

31. On which of the U.S. Caribbean islands must you drive on the left side of the road?

32. In which country is a cornmeal dish called *polenta* served?

33. In Germany, the *mark* can be divided into 100 what?

34. Estonia, Latvia and Lithuania are the 3 Baltic republics of the U.S.S.R. Two of them have very similar languages. Which is different?

35. What area is served by Le Raizet airport?

36. In what country was the polka first danced?

37. Where are you if you are walking through the teeming streets of China's most populous city?

38. In what country is Edam cheese produced?

39. Name the "new" wine served in Vienna, Austria.

40. In what city is the world famous Palace Zwinger?

...ANSWERS

31. Virgin Islands
32. Italy
33. *Pfennige*
34. Estonia
35. Guadeloupe, French West Indies
36. Czechoslovakia
37. Shanghai
38. The Netherlands
39. *Der Heurige*
40. Dresden, Germany

QUESTIONS...

41. What city are you touring if the castle of Hradcany towers above?

42. Where are you is you hear someone say *"arrivederci"* instead of "goodbye"?

43. What is the name of the Irish airline?

44. When you take the ferry from Hatteras to Ocrakcoke Island, which American state are you in?

45. In what Spanish city can you see the Cervantes house?

46. Name the architect of St. Paul's Cathedral in London, England.

47. What are the 4 official languages of Switzerland?

48. You might be served a hunter's stew called *bigos* when dining in what country?

49. What is the former capial of China, where thousands of life-size terracotta soldiers were recently discovered?

50. What country are you in if you visit the mysterious city of Timbuktu?

...ANSWERS

41. Prague, Czechoslovakia
42. Italy
43. Aer Lingus
44. North Carolina
45. Valladolid
46. Sir Christopher Wren
47. German, French, Italian, Romansch
48. Poland
49. Xi'an
50. Mali

QUESTIONS...

51. Which city in the U.S.A. lies at the highest altitude?

52. In what country can you visit King Solomon's mines?

53. Name the capital of Laos.

54. In what city is *bouillabaisse*, a French fish soup, served as the specialty?

55. In what country will the people say, *"Sayonara"* when you leave?

56. In what country did Antonio Gaudi, the outstanding art nouveau architect, work most of his life?

57. In what country is a light green wine called *verdicchio* produced?

58. What is the name of the Polish airline?

59. In what country can Kruger nature and animal preserve be seen?

60. On what Caribbean island can you visit the Carib Indians' Reservation?

51. Leadville, Colorado
52. Israel
53. Vientiane
54. Marseille
55. Japan
56. Barcelona, Spain
57. Italy
58. LOT
59. Republic of South Africa
60. Dominica, British West Indies

61. Name the African country where women warriors called *Amazons* fought in the past.

62. What are the 3 official languages of Belgium?

63. What city and country does Mingaladon airport serve?

64. *Teriyaki* originated and is still served in what country?

65. In what museum, in what city, can Botticelli's masterpiece, the *Primavera*, be admired?

66. In what U.S. state can you vacation at Myrtle Beach?

67. To what country do the Galapagos Islands, famous from Darwin's studies, belong?

68. Name the 6 smallest continental countries in Europe.

69. In what month does Oktoberfest, a beer festival in Munich, Germany, begin?

70. What country are you visiting if you buy fish 'n' chips from a street vendor?

61. Benin, Africa

62. French, Flemish, German

63. Rangoon, Myanmar (Burma)

64. Japan

65. Uffizzi Museum, Florence, Italy

66. South Carolina

67. Ecuador

68. Vatican City, San Marino, Liechtenstein, Luxembourg, Monaco, Andorra

69. September

70. England

71. The island of Sylt, a beach resort, is part of what country?

72. What city on a lake in China is famous for the beauty of its many parks?

73. Name the ancient city of the Incas in Peru.

74. What is the main avenue in Paris, known for its sidewalk cafes?

75. What are the German names of the two internationally famous health resorts in Czechoslovakia?

76. What island does hybla honey, considered the best in world by many connoisseurs, come from?

77. What great art museum can you visit on a trip to Amsterdam?

78. In which country is *paella*, a rice dish with fish or meat, a specialty?

79. What volcano covered Pompeii with lava in ancient times, and can be explored today?

80. What is the northernmost European capital?

71. Germany
72. Hangzhou
73. Cuzco
74. Champs Elysees
75. Carlsbad, Marienbad
76. Sicily, Italy
77. Rijkmuseum
78. Spain
79. Mt. Vesuvius
80. Reykjavik, Iceland

81. In what country is Eliat, one of the most beautiful seaside resorts in the Middle East?

82. Where could you visit the Lock Museum of America, with over 22,000 locks, including a replica of the oldest Egyptian device?

83. What country produces more than 50% of the world's cork?

84. Where can you visit the ruins of Chichenitze?

85. Where in Florida can you see the house of the American novelist, Ernest Hemingway?

86. Athletes from all over the world traveled to the capital of Bosnia for the 1984 Winter Olympics. Name the city.

87. In what region of France is *Camembert* cheese produced?

88. In what city in the Soviet Union can you visit the Tretyakov Gallery, an art museum?

89. On what island can the ruins of the Palace of Knossos be seen?

90. What was the African country Zaire formerly named?

...ANSWERS

81. Israel
82. Terryville, Connecticut
83. Portugal
84. Merida, Mexico
85. Key West
86. Sarajevo, Yugoslavia
87. Normandy
88. Moscow
89. Crete, Greece
90. Belgian Congo

QUESTIONS...

91. What city are you visiting if you hear the strains of the annual Wagner festival?

92. What French city is famous for its many cathedrals with beautiful stained glass windows?

93. *Chianti*, the popular Italian wine, comes from which province?

94. Where have you arrived if you are greeted with, *"Ni hao"*?

95. What French health resort was the country's capital for part of World War II?

96. Name the country famous for its spectacular fjords.

97. When visiting Krakow you can stand on the banks of what river?

98. If you want to go to Moscow, but can only travel in the U.S.A., how many states could you visit?

99. Name India's best known monument, built for a princess.

100. What country serves *cous-cous* as a popular main dish?

91. Bayreuth, West Germany

92. Troyes

93. Tuscany

94. China

95. Vichy

96. Norway

97. Vistula

98. 12: Arkansas, Idaho, Indiana, Kansas, Kentucky, Michigan, Mississippi, Ohio, Pennsylvania, Tennessee, Texas, Vermont

99. Taj Mahal

100. Tunisia

101. When Europeans first traveled to New Zealand, what native people were living there?

102. Monegasques are the citizens of what country?

103. In what country can you see the ruins of the ancient city of Pagan?

104. The Swedes celebrate the crayfish season with many parties and festivities. What is the official date for the start of this season?

105. What is the name of the most famous French restaurant in Vienne, France?

106. Name the country whose bakeries can carry over 100 kinds of bread.

107. What European country is called the "Emerald Isle"?

108. Name the 3 major airports serving the New York metropolitan area.

109. Name the main shopping street in Shanghai, China.

110. TAP is which country's airline?

101. Maori
102. Monaco
103. Myanmar (Burma)
104. 8 August
105. Les Pyramides
106. Germany
107. Ireland
108. J.F. Kennedy, La Guardia, Newark (N.J.)
109. Nanking Road
110. Portugal

QUESTIONS...

111. In what part of France are you if you are driving along Le Chemin du Tabac, the Tobacco Road?

112. The Kunsthalle in Hamburg, Germany, is known for its paintings by Meister Francke. In what other city can the works of this medieval painter be seen?

113. What is the name of Amsterdam's airport?

114. What do these have in common: Beaver, Raccoon, Skunk, Seal and Russian?

115. What city is known for its Romanesque sculptures of Antelami and its superb ham and cheese?

116. In what country can you enjoy the delicate flavor and aroma of *avgolemono* soup?

117. Where in the U.S.A. can the magnificent Yosemite Park be visited?

118. In what Polish city can you see the icon of the Black Madonna?

119. El Greco's house and museum can be visited in the city where the painter spent most of his life. Name it.

120. What country are you in if you are in the capital city of N'Djamena?

111. Southwest
112. Helsinki, Finland
113. Schiphol
114. They are all North American rivers
115. Parma, Italy
116. Greece
117. California
118. Czestochowa
119. Toledo, Spain
120. Chad

QUESTIONS...

121. Rochambeau Bridge spans which river?

122. As you leave which country are you bade, *"Dowidzenia"*?

123. In what German city can you visit Beck's brewery?

124. What is the name of the largest park in Tokyo, Japan?

125. What is the former name of Ulianowsk, the birthplace of Lenin?

126. Pick this flower in Romania, where it is called "serpent's eye", or pick it in the U.S.A., where it has a more endearing name–what?

127. In what country can you see the ruins of Persepolis, a city built in the 5th century B.C., by Darius the Great?

128. Name the island where the tail-less cat, the manx, originated.

129. What is the smallest Canadian province?

130. The geographic center of North America lies in which of the United States?

121. Potomac
122. Poland
123. Bremen
124. Ueno
125. Simbirsk
126. Forget-me-not
127. Iran
128. Isle of Man
129. Prince Edward Island
130. North Dakota

131. What is the name of the famous castle in Krakow, Poland?

132. While visiting the French West Indies, you will notice that Creole is spoken on every island except one on which you will hear a Norman dialect. Name this island.

133. In what city can you visit the Phillips Gallery?

134. In Rwanda, Africa, the Pygmies live alongside a people whose height averages at least 6 feet. Who are they?

135. When in Iraq, you are in the territory of which ancient land?

136. On which island can you meet the descendants of the Ainus Caucasian people, the first inhabitants of what is now Japan?

137. In what country is *Marimara* wine served?

138. In what city can you visit El Prado museum?

139. In what country is chopped meat with garlic and onion, called *booz*, a specialty?

140. What is the decorated footwear which Eskimos sport?

131. Wawel
132. St. Barthelmy
133. Washington, D.C.
134. The Watusi
135. Mesopotamia
136. Hokkaido
137. Turkey
138. Madrid, Spain
139. Outer Mongolia
140. *Mukluk*

QUESTIONS...

141. In what city can a large statue of Roland (11th century) be seen in front of the Rathaus?

142. What museum in Paris is especially known for its collection of impressionist art?

143. In what country can you tour the dairies that make Stilton cheese?

144. What Spanish town draws thousands of Christian pilgrims to the Virgin Mary each year?

145. Which country's inhabitants are sometimes called "Kiwis", a name derived from a flightless bird?

146. What is the largest resort on the Pacific coast of Mexico?

147. In what country can the ruins of Angkor Wat be seen?

148. Name the tallest mountain in Africa.

149. In what country is "Bird's Nest Soup" served as a delicacy?

150. What country grows tobacco called *latakiah*?

...ANSWERS

141. Bremen, Germany
142. Gare d'Orsay
143. England
144. Guadelupe
145. New Zealand
146. Acapulco
147. Kampuchea
148. Mt. Kilimanjaro
149. China
150. Syria

151. Name the biggest church in Munich, Germany.

152. What classic dramatic form might you see at a Japanese theater?

153. What meat and vegetable dish is served as a specialty in The Netherlands?

154. In what city can you see Napoleon's family house?

155. How many republics are there in the Soviet Union?

156. Where can you see the renowned Blue Grotto?

157. Name an African city with a street called Champs Elysee and a park called Bois du Boulogne.

158. In what country can you enjoy the spa waters of the hot spring at Beppu?

159. What is the third largest English-speaking country?

160. Name the largest Catholic cathedral you will find in New York State.

151. Frauekirche
152. *Kabuki* or *Noh*
153. *Hutspot*
154. Ajaccio, Corsica
155. Fifteen
156. Capri, Italy
157. Ouagadougou, Burkina Faso
158. Japan
159. The Philippines
160. St. Patrick's, New York City

161. For what is the French village of Nuits St-Georges most famous?

162. In what country can the ruins and caves of Cappadocia be seen?

163. Of what city is Via Veneto the main shopping street?

164. Name the most popular river tour for viewing German towns and castles.

165. What valley in the U.S.A. is best known for its quality wines?

166. If you visit the old city of Ragusa on the Adriatic coast, where would you go today?

167. The Caribbean island of Hispaniola is shared by what 2 countries?

168. What are the lovely slippers that you can purchase in the noisy markets of Morocco?

169. What is the Romanian specialty of grilled minced meat, served as sausages?

170. Mas a Terra, one of the Juan Fernandez Islands, inspired Defoe to write the Robinson Crusoe story. What country is it part of?

161. Wine
162. Turkey
163. Rome, Itlay
164. The Rhine Excursion
165. Napa Valley, California
166. Dubrovnik, Yugoslavia
167. Haiti and the Dominican Republic
168. *Babouches*
169. *Mititei*
170. Chile

171. In what city can you visit Alhambra?

172. Of which country was Siam-Reap the ancient capital?

173. Cock-a-leekie is a soup native to what part of Great Britain?

174. What trees is Lebanon most famous for?

175. Name a city in Florida which specializes in the production of cigars.

176. If you order a rehoboam of champagne, it would contain the equivalent of how many bottles?

177. What is the former British colony of Rhodesia called now?

178. In what city can Albrecht Durer house, a well-preserved burgher house, be seen?

179. The inhabitants of which country call it the "Land of the Morning Calm"?

180. Public notices in Yugoslavia are repeated in which 5 languages?

171. Grenada, Spain

172. Kampuchea

173. Scotland

174. Cedar

175. Tampa

176. Six

177. Zimbabwe

178. Nuremburg, Germany

179. Korea

180. Albanian, Hungarian, Macedonian, Serbo-Croatian, Slovenian

QUESTIONS...

181. What 2 islands can be seen off the coast of Amalfi?

182. Name this ancient city: capital of Japan before Tokyo.

183. Between what cities can you ride the Blue Train, the last of the world's luxury trains?

184. St.Mark's Cathedral, built in Byzantine style, can be visited in which country?

185. In what country can Tikal, the oldest Mayan ruins, be seen?

186. Bordeaux wine can be bought in bottles equivalent to 8 standard bottles. What is the large bottle called?

187. What town has as its landmark the tower from which Galileo made his discoveries?

188. Name a New York State spa known for both its waters and its horse-racing.

189. What castle can be seen in the heart of Moscow?

190. What is the most sacred and celebrated mountain in Japan?

181. Capri, Ischia

182. Kyoto

183. Pretoria and Cape Town, Republic of South Africa

184. Venice, Italy

185. Guatemala

186. Imperial

187. Pisa, Italy

188. Saratoga Springs

189. Kremlin

190. Mt. Fuji

QUESTIONS...

191. In what city can you see Frederick the Great's castle, Sans Souci?

192. Name the largest city in Israel.

193. What town is the "Corncob Capital of the World"–named for the pipes it produces?

194. Which German spa in the Black Forest is famed for its casino?

195. If you order the Czech national dish, what will you be served?

196. In what city can you climb the Spanish Steps?

197. Ernest Hemingway wrote *Farewell to Arms* in a two-story barn in the town of Piggott. Where is Piggott?

198. A 19th-century iron tower is a landmark of which European capital?

199. Where do you see opera in London?

200. The ruins of the mysterious city of Palmyra can be seen in which country?

191. Potsdam, Germany
192. Tel Aviv
193. Washington, Missouri, U.S.A.
194. Baden-Baden
195. *Knedliky*
196. Rome
197. Arkansas, U.S.A.
198. Paris, France (Eiffel Tower)
199. Covent Garden
200. Lebanon

QUESTIONS...

201. In what country is *Kronenbourg* beer brewed?

202. What European town is sought for its many Byzantine mosaics?

203. Sea Island is in which U.S. state?

204. *Sauerbrauten* is the specialty beef dish of what country?

205. Name the repertory theater in Paris.

206. What 3 African countries have names beginning with "z"?

207. Where can you visit the Pierpont Morgan Library with one of the world's best collections of medieval manuscripts?

208. What modern country is home of the ancient city of Babylon?

209. In what country can you see the Pyramid of Cheops?

210. Near what city in Israel will you find the well known sulphur springs?

201. France
202. Ravenna, Italy
203. Georgia
204. Germany
205. La Comedie Francaise
206. Zaire, Zambia, Zimbabwe
207. New York City
208. Iraq
209. Egypt
210. Tiberias

QUESTIONS...

211. What place is known as "Fragrant Harbor"?

212. *Caldeirada a pescadora* is a fish stew served in what country?

213. In what city can you tour La Brera art museum?

214. Shqiperia is a European country known as what to English-speaking people?

215. Name the oldest restaurant in Philadelphia, Pennsylvania.

216. The Statue of Liberty stands in what body of water?

217. Where in Israel can you see the "battlefield of many nations"?

218. Name 2 countries inhabited by Basques.

219. Banos de Jahuel, 4,000 feet above sea level, is a health resort in which South American country?

220. What country contains 60,000 lakes and has 30,000 islands off its shores?

211. Hong Kong
212. Portugal
213. Milan, Italy
214. Albania
215. Bookbinder's
216. New York Bay
217. Megiddo
218. France, Spain
219. Chile
220. Finland

QUESTIONS...

221. In what city can you see over 20,000 wind-mills–more than in any other city in the world?

222. What German city has for centuries been known for its china?

223. Which museum is one of the main attractions of Istanbul?

224. Name the major Polish spa in the Carpathian mountains.

225. If you order a jeroboam each of champagne and bordeaux wine, you will get the equivalent of how many bottles of each?

226. What are the 2 official languages of South Africa?

227. Name the oldest university town in Hungary.

228. In what museum in what city can you see the original of Leonardo da Vinci's painting *La Gioconda*?

229. The Russian *ruble* can be divided into 100 what?

230. What is the present name of the former German colony of Southwest Africa?

221. Merida, Mexico
222. Meissen
223. Topkapi
224. Krynica
225. Champagne–4; bordeaux–6
226. Afrikaans, English
227. Pecs
228. The Louvre, Paris
229. *Kopecks*
230. Namibia

QUESTIONS...

231. What was Taiwan formerly called?

232. Name a French resort and spa on Lake Geneva known for the special properties of its waters.

233. What is Africa's most easterly point?

234. In what Belgian town are *boudins blancs aux raisins* (white sausages with grapes) the specialty?

235. While touring what city can you visit the museum Dahlem Gemaeldegallerie?

236. Name the largest of the Channel Islands.

237. What city was once the capital of Russian territories in America?

238. Name Portugal's famed beach resort.

239. Where can Spinoza's house be seen?

240. In what country can you visit the ruins of the ancient city of Ba'albek with the temple of Heliopitan Jupiter?

231. Formosa
232. Evian
233. Cape Guardafui
234. Audenarde
235. Berlin
236. Jersey
237. Sitka, Alaska
238. Estoril
239. The Hague, The Netherlands
240. Lebanon

241. In France it is called *tapis roulant* (rolling carpet); in Germany, *Laufband* (running strip); in English?

242. Near what city is the palace of Nymphenburg?

243. Rehoboth Beach is a resort in what U.S. state?

244. Burgundy wine can be baought in bottles equivalent to 8 standard bottles. What is this large bottle called?

245. In what country is Byblos, the city from which the word "bible" is derived?

246. What former Byzantine cathedral was converted to a mosque in Istanbul?

247. The largest lake in Hungary is unsurpassed in Central Europe. Name it.

248. What French city produces most of the country's china?

249. Name the opera house in Milan, Italy.

250. What city was the boyhood home of Mark Twain?

241. Moving walkway
242. Munich, Germany
243. Delaware
244. Methuselah
245. Lebanon
246. Hagia Sophia
247. Lake Balaton
248. Limoges
249. La Scala
250. Hannibal, Missouri, U.S.A.

QUESTIONS...

251. In what country is *churrasco*, meat roasted on an open flame, a specialty?

252. Devil's Island is part of what country?

253. If you walk under a triumphal arch named Brandenburger Tor, what city are you visiting?

254. Name the city in southern France famed for the production of perfume.

255. The graceful landmark of Copenhagen is a statue of what?

256. What city in the U.S.A. attracts thousands of tourists to its annual carnival celebrations?

257. Name a country spread over 7,100 islands.

258. Through which 6 countries does the river Danube flow?

259. The ruins of which ancient circus still draw visitors to Rome?

260. What British colony lies at the entrance to the Mediterranean?

...ANSWERS

251. Brazil

252. French Guiana

253. Berlin

254. Grasse

255. Mermaid

256. New Orleans, Louisiana

257. The Philippines

258. Austria, Czechoslovakia, Germany, Hungary, Romania, Yugoslavia

259. Circus Maximus

260. Gibraltar

261. Name the Egyptian temple city near Luxor.

262. Which 3 Baltic states are now republics of the Soviet Union?

263. What is the delicious salad of avocado and onions made in Mexico?

264. St. Peter's Basilica can be toured in what country?

265. Name the largest lake between Switzerland and Italy.

266. Which is the 11th-century gate at the entrance to Ingolstadt, Germany?

267. What are the capitals of Greek and Yugoslav Macedonia?

268. In what city will you find the Frick Gallery?

269. You would most likely start a trip to Tasmania in its capital city. What is it called?

270. In what city can you visit Rembrandt's house?

261. Karnak
262. Estonia, Latvia, Lithuania
263. *Guacamole*
264. Vatican City
265. Como
266. Kreuztor
267. Thessaloniki, Skopje
268. New York
269. Hobart
270. Amsterdam, The Netherlands

271. What canal connects the Red and the Mediterranean seas?

272. Name the bathroom fixture found in most French hotels but practically never in American or English ones.

273. Tripe in tomato sauce is a specialty of which French town?

274. Name the 2 famous spas in the Soviet Union, both in the foothills of the Caucasian mountains.

275. In what city will you find the Place de la Concorde?

276. The West Frisian Islands are part of what country?

277. Name William Faulkner's native town, where his house can now be visited.

278. Where is Westminster cathedral?

279. The Kalahari desert is on what continent?

280. The most revered center of Islam in Tunisia is in which town?

271. Suez Canal
272. Bidet
273. Caen
274. Kislovodsk, Pyatigorsk
275. Paris, France
276. The Netherlands
277. Oxford, Mississippi
278. London, England
279. Africa
280. Kairouan

281. What Caribbean island is famous for its phosphorescent bay?

282. In what country are curries called *kaeng phed* a specialty?

283. What Catholic pilgrimage center is in the French Pyrenees?

284. One of the greatest medieval paintings is Gruenewald's *Crucifixion*. Where can you see the original?

285. Near what city can you see the fabulous palace of Schoenbrunn?

286. What American beach is famous for auto racing?

287. What is the capital of The Netherlands?

288. *Barberi* is a flat bread baked in which country?

289. What is the name for carnival in Munich, Germany?

290. Hyde Park is a beautifully landscaped area open to those in which city?

281. Puerto Rico
282. Thailand
283. Lourdes
284. Colmar, France
285. Vienna, Austria
286. Daytona Beach, Florida
287. Amsterdam
288. Iran
289. *Fasching*
290. London, England

QUESTIONS...

291. Name the famous theater in Vienna, Austria.

292. The San Blas Islands are part of which country?

293. In his travelog *A Tramp Abroad* Mark Twain called this country "simply a large, humpy, solid rock with a thin skin of grass stretched over it." Name it.

294. In what country is *Barak Palinka*, an apricot brandy, made?

295. Name the mountain resort near Rio de Janeiro, with the Museum of the Empire.

296. What is the specialty meal in all Scandinavian countries?

297. Visitors to Romania can enjoy the country's largest beach. Name it.

298. Name the best known Chinese beer, brewed in a former German colony from the early 20th century.

299. In what city is Picadilly Circus a busy intersection?

300. The snowcapped Tatra Mountains form the border between which 2 countries?

...ANSWERS

291. Burg Theater
292. Panama
293. Switzerland
294. Hungary
295. Petropolis, Brazil
296. *Smorgasbord*
297. Mamaia Beach
298. *Tsing Tao*
299. London, England
300. Poland, Czechoslovakia

301. What is spice is the hallmark of Hungarian cooking?

302. *Kvas*, a non-alcoholic drink of the U.S.S.R., is usually made from what staple?

303. What is the most popular beach in New York State?

304. What Belgian city is renowned for its carnival celebrations?

305. To whom is the main cathedral in Vienna, Austria dedicated?

306. What city are you visiting if you drive under the imposing Arc de Triomphe?

307. Name the great African waterfalls, twice as high and twice as wide as Niagara Falls.

308. The Gobi Desert extends through which 2 countries?

309. There is an island off of China which is a Portuguese dependency. Name it.

310. What zoo has the world's largest collection of animals?

301. Paprika
302. Bread
303. Jones Beach, Long Island
304. Binche
305. St. Stefan
306. Paris, France
307. Victoria Falls, Zimbabwe
308. China, Mongolia
309. Macao
310. San Diego Zoo, San Diego, California

QUESTIONS...

311. By what name do you order a Polish vodka flavored with bison grass?

312. The Turtle Islands are part of what archipelago in what country?

313. Travelers have said of that "you can die after you have seen" this beautiful city. Name it.

314. In what mountain range will you find the tiny country of Andorra?

315. *Ngapi-htaung* is a fish dish served with boiled potatoes. In what country is it the staple food?

316. If you enter the Panama Canal from the Atlantic Ocean and exit into the Pacific, will you be east or west of your starting point?

317. What South American city is famous for its carnival festivities?

318. What national historic landmark is one of the oldest seashore resorts on the U.S. Atlantic coast?

319. Kathmandu is the capital of what country?

320. What is the most populous city in Africa?

311. *Zubrowka*
312. Sulu archipelago, The Philippines
313. Naples, Italy
314. The Pyrenees
315. Myanmar (Burma)
316. East
317. Rio de Janeiro, Brazil
318. Cape May, New Jersey
319. Nepal
320. Cairo, Egypt

QUESTIONS...

321. Name the South Atlantic island where Napoleon was exiled.

322. Srinagar is a city with more miles of canal than of road. It is the capital of what state in India?

323. Near what lake is the Italian wine *Bardolino* produced?

324. What is the name of the most famous beach at Honolulu, Hawaii?

325. In what country will you hear *fado* music?

326. Where in Mexico is the "silver city"?

327. If you decided to have a case of champagne in a single bottle, what would you order?

328. What country covers 13,000 islands?

329. In what country might you be served *locro*, a soup made with corn, potatoes, and cheese?

330. Name the largest and busiest harbor in Belgium.

321. St. Helena
322. Kashmir
323. Garda
324. Waikiki
325. Portugal
326. Taxco
327. Salmanazar
328. Indonesia
329. Ecuador
330. Antwerp

QUESTIONS...

331. What is considered the best fortified town on earth?

332. Where can you visit the Chopin museum and house?

333. The *lira* is the monetary unit of which 4 countries?

334. Name a metropolis divided between Europe and Asia.

335. Name the highest waterfalls in South America.

336. What is the name of Chicago's international airport?

337. Mozart composed *Don Giovanni* in the Bertram Villa in which city?

338. At the Bacardi Museum you can see a collection of Indian relics and exhibits on rum making. Where is it?

339. What is the largest city in Pakistan?

340. Which modern capital stands on the site of a Hittite settlement?

331. Valetta, Malta
332. Zelazna Wola, Poland
333. Italy, San Marino, Turkey, Vatican City
334. Istanbul
335. Angel Falls, Venezuela
336. O'Hare
337. Prague, Czechoslovakia
338. Santiago, Cuba
339. Karachi
340. Ankara, Turkey

341. Which is the world's oldest seaport city?

342. What is the tallest free-standing structure, and where can you see it?

343. There is a sacred monkey forest in Sanjeh on what island?

344. What country's national unit of currency is the *forint*?

345. In what city can a Roman bridge across the Guadalquivir still be seen today?

346. Name the walled medieval city on the river Tauber, in Germany.

347. In what U.S. state will you find the Mammoth Cave?

348. What is the name of the art museum in Munich, Germany?

349. What city is the commercial and financial center of Australia?

350. Which country is the original home of coffee?

...ANSWERS

341. Jaffa in Tel Aviv, Israel
342. C.N. Tower, Toronto, Canada
343. Bali
344. Hungary
345. Cordoba, Spain
346. Rothenburg
347. Kentucky
348. Pinakothek
349. Melbourne
350. Ethiopia

351. *Kirsch* is a hard liquor produced mainly in France and Germany. What is the basic ingredient?

352. Portela is the airport for what city?

353. Name the London museum famous for its collection of paintings by J.M. Turner.

354. In what city is a mad carnival called *Moomba* celebrated for 10 days in March?

355. In what city can you see the Doge's Palace?

356. What is the only man-made structure that can be seen from the moon?

357. Where in the U.S. can you see a tank museum?

358. Name the area where 3 mountain ranges meet: the Himalayas, the Karakoram, and the Hindu Kush.

359. There is only one language in the world related to Basque, and it is spoken in 2 principalities. Name the language, the principalities, and their country.

360. In which city is the Kentucky Derby run each year?

351. Cherries

352. Lisbon, Portugal

353. Tate Gallery

354. Melbourne, Australia

355. Venice, Italy

356. Great Wall, China

357. Aberdeen, Maryland

358. Kafiristan, Pakistan

359. Brusheski; spoken in Hunza and Nagar, Pakistan

360. Louisville, Kentucky

QUESTIONS...

361. Which is the deepest freshwater lake in the world?

362. Name the Moscow museum housing a fine collection of international masters.

363. Forest Hills, in the New York borough of Queens, draws thousands of spectators to its international competition in which sport?

364. It is a country's capital, but it is best known for its casino. Name this city.

365. What is the major seaside resort near London, England with a pavilion built in an Indian mode?

366. What is the capital of Greenland?

367. Visitors to Venice want to walk across what famous store-lined bridge?

368. In what country is *skyr*, a dish of milk curds, popular?

369. Name the only walled city in North America.

370. What is the most famous beach on Bali?

361. Lake Baikal, Siberia
362. Pushkin Art Museum
363. Tennis
364. Monte Carlo
365. Brighton
366. Godthaab
367. Rialto
368. Iceland
369. Quebec, Canada
370. Kuta

371. What city with 400 temples is known as the "City of Angels"?

372. A tour of London should include the royal palace. What is it called?

373. In what U.S. state can the public now visit Hearst Castle?

374. A Russian Orthodox cathedral, a replica of St. Basil's, Moscow, surpises you in what French city?

375. What is the currency of Bulgaria?

376. In what town can you visit Peace Memorial Park?

377. Freedom Square is the principal square of what city?

378. In what city is the Shalom Meir Tower, tallest building in the Middle East?

379. Which southeast Asian country was never colonized?

380. In what city can you visit Dvorjak's house called Villa America?

371. Bangkok, Thailand
372. Buckingham Palace
373. California
374. Nice
375. *Lev*
376. Hiroshima, Japan
377. Valetta, Malta
378. Tel Aviv, Israel
379. Thailand
380. Prague, Czechoslovakia

QUESTIONS...

381. Why must you change trains when traveling by rail between France and Spain?

382. Name the 6 New England states of the U.S.A.

383. Name the main cathedral in Paris.

384. What Middle Eastern city was formerly called Philadelphia?

385. In what South American countries can you visit the shores of both Atlantic and Pacific oceans?

386. Where is the lowest point on earth?

387. To what city have you sailed if you are docked in the world's highest floating harbor?

388. Name the hiking trail running through most of the eastern seaboard of the U.S.A.

389. What country are you entering if you land at Keflavik international airport?

390. The Austrian monetary unit is the *schilling*. It can be divided into 100 what?

381. Spanish gauges are broader than French

382. Connecticut, Maine, Massachusetts, New Hampshire, Rhode Island, Vermont

383. Notre Dame

384. Amman, Jordan

385. Colombia, Chile

386. Dead Sea (between Israel and Jordan)

387. Manaus, Brazil

388. Appalachian Trail

389. Iceland

390. *Groschen*

391. In what country is Goyllarisquisga, with the world's highest coal mine?

392. Which museum in Krakow, Poland displays paintings by Rembrandt and Leonardo da Vinci?

393. There are 2 islands in the river Seine in Paris. Name them.

394. What city is considered the oldest continually inhabited urban settlement?

395. Which Caribbean island belongs to Colombia?

396. Name a volcano recently active in the U.S.A.

397. If you choose to visit the biggest city in South America where would you go?

398. Name the museum where you can see a 17th-century warship recovered from the sea in 1961.

399. In Australia you can see one of the most impressive of nature's wonders–a rock with a circumference greater than 5 miles. What is it called?

400. What is the castle built by William the Conqueror in the vicinity of London, and now open to visitors?

391. Peru
392. Czartoryski
393. Ile St. Louis, Ile de la Cite
394. Damascus, Syria
395. St. Andres
396. Mt. St. Helens, Washington
397. Sao Paulo, Brazil
398. Vasa Museum, Stockholm, Sweden
399. Ayres Rock (Mt. Olga National Park)
400. Windsor Castle

QUESTIONS...

401. Where can you visit the Mormon church's temple and tabernacle?

402. What is Canada's largest city?

403. Where should you go to see the square architecturally the most beautiful in the world?

404. What is the museum in Kansas City, Missouri housing a famous collection of Oriental art?

405. What people enjoy *blini*, buckwheat pancakes served with sour cream, melted butter, herring, and caviar?

406. Name the southernmost tip of South America.

407. Which Scottish island is famous for the production of wool?

408. Where is the most modern Mexican beach resort, within sight of Isla de las Mujeres?

409. In what Chinese city did the ancient Silk Road originate?

410. The Finnish *markka* can be divided into 100 what?

401. Salt Lake City, Utah, U.S.A.
402. Montreal, Quebec
403. Grande Place, Brussels, Belgium
404. Nelson-Atkins Museum of Fine Art
405. Russians
406. Cape Horn
407. Shetland
408. Cancun
409. Xi'an
410. *Pennia*

QUESTIONS...

411. Which city is refered to as the "Big Apple"?

412. Name the ancient seat of government at Athens, whose ruins can still be seen today.

413. What is the holiest city in Iran, a pilgrimage center for Shi'ite moslems.

414. Name the luxury hotel built at the turn of the century which was used for filming *Some Like It Hot*, starring Marilyn Monroe.

415. To what area would you travel to purchase a beautiful Kazak carpet?

416. What square is the focal point of modern Cairo?

417. In what Roman piazza can you see 3 fountains by Bernini?

418. Where in China will you find a restaurant which can seat 9,000 people at a time? What is it called?

419. In what French town can you see many memorials and museums of the battles of World War I?

420. Where can you watch a day-long performance of a Passion Play, once in 10 years?

411. New York
412. Acropolis
413. Meshed (Mashhad)
414. Hotel Del Coronado, California
415. Caucasus
416. Tahrir
417. Piazza Navona
418. Beijing (Peking), Beijing Duck
419. Verdun
420. Oberammergau, Germany

QUESTIONS...

421. What was the 9th century capital of England that later became capital of the Danish empire?

422. Name the romantic vehicles you can ride on the canals of Venice.

423. What is the largest island in the world?

424. About what Norwegian city is it said that "if a horse sees a man without an umbrella it takes fright?"

425. Which Swedish city is served by Landvetter airport?

426. Where can you see one hundred $10,000 bills on display?

427. What is the name of the Belgian airline?

428. Name the country where you can see the most monuments of Abbasid art.

429. What is the famous London pub named after a fictional detective?

430. Name the variety music hall made famous by the paintings of Toulouse-Lautrec.

421. Winchester
422. Gondolas
423. Greenland
424. Bergen
425. Gothenburg
426. Binton's Horseshoe Club, Las Vegas, Nevada
427. Sabena
428. Iraq
429. The Sherlock Holmes
430. Moulin Rouge

431. Name the French-speaking province in Canada.

432. Gulbenkian, once considered the richest man in the world, established the Gulbenkian Center for Arts and Culture. Where can you visit it?

433. In Copenhagen you can visit 2 breweries of famous Danish beers. What are they?

434. What is Australia's biggest horseracing event.

435. Which Caribbean island with a popular beach resort is part of Venezuela?

436. How many United Arab Emirates are there?

437. In what southern French city can you visit the Chagall Museum?

438. Name the main shopping street in Los Angeles, California.

439. What is the name of the Spanish monastery built for Philip II?

440. In what country will you hear gypsy music played in restaurants?

431. Quebec
432. Lisbon, Portugal
433. Tuborg, Carlsberg
434. The Melbourne Cup
435. Santa Margherita
436. Seven
437. Nice
438. Wilshire Boulevard
439. Escorial
440. Hungary

441. In what American city can you visit the Isabella Stewart Gardener Museum?

442. What is the oldest national park in Canada?

443. In what country is *cuchuco*, a thick barley and meat soup served with peppercorns, the specialty?

444. What is the capital of Soviet Georgia?

445. Which 2 states in the U.S.A. have cities named Bedford, Columbus and Washington?

446. The currency of Nepal, the *rupee*, can be divided into 100 what?

447. Vaclavske Nemesti is the principal square of what city?

448. In what city will you find the Big Wild Goose Pagoda and the Small Wild Goose Pagoda?

449. Name the pancake snack eaten in South India.

450. What do these names have in common: Jackson, Jefferson, Levy, Madison, Monroe, Washington?

441. Boston, Massachusetts
442. Banff in the Rocky Mountains
443. Colombia
444. Tbilisi
445. Indiana, Ohio
446. *Paisas*
447. Prague, Czechoslovakia
448. Xi'an, China
449. *Dosai*
450. All counties in Florida, U.S.A.

451. Name the oldest city in Siberia, founded in 1585.

452. Malatesta, a wealthy Italian, built his mistress a Renaissance temple called Tempio Malatestiano. Where can you see it?

453. *Matte* is the specialty dish of one of the Caribbean islands; it is a fricasse of land crab on rice spiced with red pepper. Where can you eat it?

454. In what city is the Porta Nigra, one of the best preserved gates from the late Roman empire?

455. What swimming attire is named after an island?

456. Which is the largest library in the world?

457. Where was Napoleon lost in a maze?

458. Research has not yet established which of these rivers is the longest in the world. Name both.

459. In what city was the Synagogue de la Paix constructed in 1958?

460. A popular song begins, 'I left my heart in" what city?

451. Tyumen
452. Rimini, Italy
453. St. Bartholomew
454. Trier, Germany
455. Bikini
456. U.S. Library of Congress, Washington, D.C.
457. Stra, Italy
458. Amazon, Nile
459. Strasbourg, France
460. San Francisco

461. Name the art museums in Oxford and Cambridge, England.

462. What country would you visit to see the Dunhang grottoes on the old Silk Road?

463. Where can you see the Frans Hals museum?

464. What is the highest peak in Europe, and in what mountain range is it?

465. Of what style of art is the Universidad Nacional Autonoma de Mexico a celebrated example?

466. What is the Italian name for the Brenner Pass?

467. Where in Germany can you visit the Gutenberg Museum?

468. Which is the only country apart from the U.S.A. whose capital is named after an American president?

469. What city gave coffee its name?

470. Name the 5 boroughs of New York City.

461. Ashmolean Gallery, Fitzwilliam Museum
462. China
463. Haarlem, The Netherlands
464. Mt. Elbrus, Caucasus mountains
465. Mosaic
466. Brennero
467. Mainz
468. Liberia (Monrovia)
469. Kaffa, Ethiopia
470. Bronx, Brooklyn, Manhattan, Queens, Richmond (Staten Island)

471. Name a baroque monastery on the river Danube.

472. Port wine is drunk all over the world, but comes from a region on what Portuguese river?

473. In what South American city was an opera house modeled on the Paris Opera?

474. Which street has the names of performing artists embedded in its sidewalk?

475. Name the city and country served by Maiquetia airport.

476. How is the imperial palace in Beijing popularly known?

477. The highest navigable body of water is Lake Titicaca. It lies 12,000 feet above sea level in what country?

478. In what Canadian city is the National Gallery?

479. In what country can you enjoy a view of Katajuta, called by the local people "mountain of many heads"?

480. What was the former name of J.F. Kennedy Airport in New York?

471. Melk
472. Douro
473. Manaus, Brazil
474. Hollywood Boulevard, Hollywood, California
475. Caracas, Venezuela
476. Forbidden City
477. Peru
478. Ottawa (capital of Canada)
479. Australia
480. Idlewild

481. In what city is Smetana's house, where he composed *Moldau*?

482. The currency of Norway, *krone*, can be divided into 100 what?

483. The capital of a Soviet republic is also one of the oldest towns in the world, founded in 783 B.C. Name the town and the republic.

484. Name Australia's airline.

485. What building in Paris is modeled after St. Peter's in Rome?

486. What 2 cities in France and Great Britain are closest?

487. What city does Ferihegy airport serve?

488. How many varieties of humming bird can be seen in the U.S.A.?

489. One of India's most unusual art treasures is carved grottoes on an island by Bombay. What is it called?

490. What was the colonial capital of Virginia, now restored for visitors?

...ANSWERS

481. Prague, Czechoslovakia
482. *Ore*
483. Yerevan, Armenia
484. Quantas
485. Les Invalides
486. Calais, France; Dover, England
487. Budapest, Hungary
488. One
489. Elephanta
490. Williamsburg

QUESTIONS...

491. Where in Germany is the Olympic City?

492. The ruins of the first synagogue built in the western hemisphere, Beracha Ve Shalom, can be seen in what country?

493. Which is the largest volcano in the world?

494. What composer is the Figaro Museum dedicated to? Where can you visit it?

495. Cousin Island was purchased by the International Council for Bird Preservation in 1968. To what island group does this birdwatcher's mecca belong?

496. Where can you visit the largest private house in the world, with 250 rooms?

497. What is the best place in the U.S.A. to study Byzantine art? Name the building and the city.

498. A special chicken dish named after its Italian city of origin was concocted for Napoleon after a battle on 14 June 1800. Name the city.

499. The oldest survivng bridge spans what river in what city?

500. What French resort on the Atlantic Ocean is closest to the Spanish border?

491. Munich
492. Surinam
493. Mt. Kilimanjaro, Tanzania
494. Mozart; Vienna, Austria
495. The Seychelles
496. Biltmore House, Asheville, North Carolina
497. Dumbarton Oaks, Washington, D.C.
498. Marengo
499. Meles in Izmir, Turkey
500. Biarritz

QUESTIONS...

501. Which island was made famous by Gaugin's paintings?

502. In which state is Okefenokee, the largest swamp in the U.S.A.?

503. What is the native town of the legendary knight, El Cid?

504. Bhutan is a tiny kingdom dominated by castle monasteries. What are they called?

505. In what city can you sample the delectable *Sacher Torte* at the Sacher coffee house?

506. What is the smallest country in the world?

507. Wrangel and Wrangell are islands belonging to which 2 countries?

508. The Dutchman Vermeer painted only 2 landscapes: a small street scene and a townscape of his native city, considered the greatest ever produced. Which town did he depict?

509. Name the largest volcano in Europe.

510. According to Moslem tradition, after expulsion from paradise Adam settled on which island?

501. Tahiti

502. Georgia

503. Burgos, Spain

504. *Dzongs*

505. Vienna, Austria

506. Vatican City (0.17 sq. miles, population under 1,000)

507. Wrangel, U.S.S.R.; Wrangell, Alaska, U.S.A.

508. Delft, The Netherlands

509. Mt. Etna, Sicily

510. Sri Lanka

511. What is the oldest medieval town in Denmark?

512. Name the popular hard liquor made in Mexico from the agave cactus.

513. Which capital city lies almost on the equator, 9,000 feet above sea level?

514. Where can you visit the house and museum of Toulouse-Lautrec?

515. What capital city does Arlanda airport serve?

516. Name the city which Shakespeare made famous with *Romeo and Juliet*.

517. What is the trail between Haarlem and Leiden in The Netherlands known as?

518. Which city has the steepest streets in the world?

519. Which is the largest synagogue in the world, and where is it located?

520. In what country should you expect to get splashed with water on the second day of Easter?

511. Ribe
512. *Tequila*
513. Quito, Ecuador
514. Albi, France
515. Stockholm, Sweden
516. Verona, Italy
517. Tulip Trail
518. San Francisco, California, U.S.A.
519. Temple Emmanuel, New York City, U.S.A.
520. Poland

521. *Bel Paese* means beautiful country in Italian. It is also the name of what type of food?

522. What is the currency of Thailand?

523. Name the famous old bridge in Prague, Czechoslovakia built with egg-based cement.

524. London is served by which 2 airports?

525. The 3 ancient mysterious cities of Central Asia: Bokhara, Khiva and Samarkand are in the same Soviet republic. Name it.

526. What is the largest lake in the world?

527. In what Mexican town is the Pyramid of the Sun?

528. What is the most populous urban area in the world?

529. Where is the longest stairway in the world?

530. Name a Spanish concoction of wine, fruit juices and brandy.

521. Cheese
522. *Baht*
523. Charles Bridge (Karluv Most)
524. Heathrow, Gatwick
525. Uzbekistan
526. Caspian Sea
527. Tetihuacan
528. New York City (over 16 million)
529. Spiez, Switzerland (11,674 steps)
530. *Sangria*

QUESTIONS...

531. Which town is said to be the oldest in the world?

532. The English Garden in Munich, Germany, was originally planted by a foreigner. What was his nationality?

533. Which country is the second largest, by area, in the world?

534. What are the following: Black, White, Red, Yellow, Coral?

535. An important collection of Andrew Wyeth's paintings is in a museum near his hometown, in Pennsylvania. Which town?

536. Where is the Golden Temple, the sacred shrine of the Sikhs?

537. The Bulgarians make a hard liquor called *rosa* from the petals of a special rose. Name this flower.

538. What is the name of the central square in Buenos Aires?

539. What is the busiest harbor town in western Germany?

540. What brand of bourbon cannot be purchased north of the Mason-Dixon line?

531. Jericho, Israel
532. American
533. Canada
534. Names of seas
535. Chadds Ford (Brandywine Museum)
536. Amritsar, India
537. Damascene rose
538. Plaza de Mayo
539. Rostock
540. Rebel Yell

541. Name the anise-flavored hard drink popular in Greece.

542. Name the small town where George Washington's ancestor's lived, and its closest modern city.

543. In what country can you visit Sybaris, once a rich city which gave its name to the Sybarites?

544. If you land at Kloten airport, to which city have you traveled?

545. During a siege of what German city was marzipan created?

546. What is the name of the remote, uninhabited island in the South Atlantic, owned by Norway?

547. If you find yourself in a *Schnellimbiss* in Germany, in what kind of establishment are you?

548. In what city was the first railroad station in history built?

549. One Polish castle houses 140 masterpieces of Flemish tapestry. Which castle?

550. American and Canadian Eskimo speak a language related to that of which Indians?

541. *Ouzo*

542. Washington; Newcastle, England

543. Italy

544. Zurich, Switzerland

545. Lubeck, Germany

546. Bouvet Island

547. Snack bar

548. Mount Clare, Baltimore, Maryland (January 1830)

549. Wawel Castle

550. Navajo

QUESTIONS...

551. What is the name of the main art museum in Venice, Italy?

552. Name the 4 Soviet Republics in Central Asia.

553. Charles de Gaulle is the main international airport of Paris, France. Name the other 2.

554. Which is the largest island in South America?

555. In which country can you visit the Garamba National Park, famous for the largest mountain gorillas; as well as the Salonga National Park, famous for its pygmy chimpanzees?

556. Wild horses roam free on 2 islands in the U.S.A. Which islands?

557. Two ancient cities were covered in lava when the volcano Vesuvius erupted. Name them.

558. On which of the Dutch West Indies can you see thousands of nesting flamingos?

559. If you wanted to watch sports events in the largest stadium in the world, where would you go?

560. Name the city that claims to be "Cowboy Capital of the World," and has the second oldest Polish parish in the U.S.A.

551. Galleria del Academia

552. Uzbek, Turkmen, Kirgiz, Tadzhik

553. Le Bourget, Orly

554. Tierra del Fuego

555. Zaire

556. Ocracoke, North Carolina; Chincoteaque, Virginia

557. Pompeii, Herculaneum

558. Bonaire

559. Strahov Stadium, Prague, Czechoslovakia

560. Bandera, Texas

561. European cars display the initials of their country when traveling abroad. F stands for France; what does FL stand for?

562. Which Israeli synagogue has stained glass windows designed by Marc Chagall?

563. Name the section of your cruise ship reserved for the crew.

564. In what city in The Netherlands can you see a house in which the Russian tsar, Peter the Great, lived?

565. What is the capital of Canada's Northwest Territories, established in 1935?

566. The earliest dam in history was built in what town?

567. In what city is the highly ceremonial Spanish Court Riding School?

568. The square of the "City of Devotees" has an ancient "bell of the barking dogs" at its center, to scare away stray dogs. Name the city.

569. Bangor is capital of the American state of Maine. Four towns in 3 European countries, each an island, have the same name. Which countries?

570. *Tavel* is a popular French rose wine. From which river basin does it come?

561. Liechtenstein

562. Haddasah Hebrew Medical Center, Jerusalem

563. Forecastle

564. Zaandem

565. Yellowknife

566. Jawa, Jordan

567. Vienna, Austria

568. Bhatgaon, Nepal

569. France, Great Britain, Ireland

570. Rhone

571. Name the railroad station which serves Philadelphia, Pennsylvania.

572. In the suburbs of what city will you find the first Gothic cathedral built in France (between 1135 and 1145)?

573. What is the name of a chain of hotels owned and run by the Spanish government?

574. What Italian brandy is made for mass consumption?

575. What city does Fuhlsbuenttel airport serve?

576. On which famous Italian beach was the body of the English poet, Keats, washed ashore in the 19th century?

577. Pablo Picasso's masterpiece depicts the first air-raid on civilians in history. In which city did it take place?

578. Which freshwater lake has the largest surface area?

579. What is the currency of Portugal?

580. *Bryndzove haluski* is whose favorite dish?

571. 30th Street Station
572. Paris (St. Denis)
573. Paradores
574. *Grappa*
575. Hamburg, Germany
576. Viareggio
577. Guernica, Spain
578. Lake Superior, U.S.A.
579. *Escudo*
580. Slovaks

581. In what country are you likely to see men in loden coats and women in dirndl dresses?

582. Which state contains the geographical center of population of the United States of America?

583. Name the oldest city in Canada.

584. Three cities in the U.S.S.R. have a house or museum dedicated to one Russian writer: Moscow, Melkhovoe (about 60 miles from Moscow) and Yalta. Who is the writer?

585. Name the Italian dessert of ice cream topped with almonds.

586. Two Caribbean islands, a few square feet in area, are separated by only a few thousand feet of water. Yet one was settled by Africans, the other by Bretons, from Normandy. What is this island group called?

587. If you stayed at the luxury Four Seasons Yalara Resort, you would be at the center of which country?

588. Which French city has one of the largest Gothic cathedrals, and frescoes by Puvis de Chavannes in its museum?

589. Where can you visit the oldest castle in the world?

590. Name the highest capital city in Africa.

581. Austria
582. Missouri
583. Quebec
584. Anton Chekhov
585. Tortoni
586. Islands of the Saints
587. Australia
588. Amiens
589. Gomdan, Yemen (built before 100 A.D.)
590. Addis Ababa, Ethiopia

591. Wagner composed some of his operas in a villa called Tribschen. In which city?

592. Which Caribbean island was the birthplace of Napoleon's wife, Josephine?

593. In The Netherlands, what is the term for land recovered from the sea?

594. The largest wooden church in the world is in the town of Kaerimeke, in which country?

595. Name the highest mountain in the U.S.A., and the state in which you can climb it.

596. What Italian city produces the world's most famous violins?

597. What are the following: Damansky, Drygalski, Lisianski, Johnston?

598. What is the present name of the country formerly known as the Gold Coast?

599. Eger, a small baroque town in Hungary, is the center of the area producing *Egri Bikaver*, a wine known to the rest of the world as what?

600. The Grand Canyon in the U.S.A. is the largest in the world. Which canyon in Eastern Europe is considered the next greatest, and is protected under a UNESCO program?

591. Luzerne, Switzerland

592. Martinique

593. *Polder*

594. Finland

595. Mount McKinley, Alaska

596. Cremona

597. Islands

598. Ghana

599. Bull's Blood

600. Canyon of the River Tara, Durmitor National Park, Yugoslavia

601. In Israel, where do Jewish people leave their prayers and petitions?

602. Name a sweet French liqueur made from blackcurrants.

603. The dormitory at M.I.T. is one of the few buildings designed by Alvar Aalto and built outside his native country. Name the country.

604. Cointrin is the airport of which city?

605. What is the best place to buy gourmet food in Moscow?

606. In what part of Italy is *osso buco* a specialty food?

607. Sankt Pauli is the entertainment quarter of which city?

608. What is the largest island in Africa?

609. What is the world's oldest stone monument, and where can you see it?

610. Where did Vincent Van Gogh live and paint during the last years of his life?

...ANSWERS

601. The Western Wall, Jerusalem
602. *Cassis*
603. Finland
604. Geneva, Switzerland
605. Gastronom #1
606. Lombardy
607. Hamburg, Germany
608. Madagascar
609. Step Pyramid, Saqqara, Egypt
610. Arles, France

611. Where can you visit the birthplace of Hans Christian Andersen?

612. Which town in Israel was the capital of King Herod the Great?

613. Failaka Island with its Greek ruins, is what country's most interesting tourist attraction?

614. An old tobacco factory, made famous by Carmen in Bizet's opera, is now a university. In which city can you visit it?

615. Where can you see the oldest painted ikon in the world?

616. Where is a truck called *Le Truck*, the vehicle of public transportation?

617. Name the popular English dish made of ri e and fish.

618. What is the most northerly town in the world?

619. Which Italian spa will cure your sore throat?

620. In what country will you see the 'Heavenly Maidens", sensuous frescoes of barebeasted women, painted fifteen centuries ago?

611. Odense, Denmark
612. Caesarea
613. Kuwait
614. Seville, Spain
615. St. Catharine, Sinai, Egypt
616. Papeete, Tahiti
617. Kedgeree
618. Hammerfest, Norway
619. Salsomaggio
620. Sri Lanka

621. A column adorns the castle square in Warsaw, Poland. To whom is it dedicated?

622. What is the oldest town in Europe, founded in 1100 B.C.?

623. *Enzian* is a popular drink in the mountains of Bavaria, Germany. What is it flavored with?

624. Which U.S. city is known for movie production?

625. Mulhouse is the airport for what city?

626. Which French town is known for growing black truffles (an extremely expensive food), as well as for gourmet dishes using black truffles?

627. In what country is a loudmouth called a *thundergub*?

628. In what Italian city are Shakespeare's plays performed in a Roman theater, about 1000 years old?

629. Where can you see the memorial to the Unknown Jewish Martyr?

630. What European capital is served by Schwechat airport?

621. King Sigismund
622. Cadiz, Spain
623. Gentian
624. Hollywood, California
625. Basel, Switzerland
626. Perigord
627. Ireland
628. Verona
629. Paris, France
630. Vienna, Austria

631. What is the largest country in the world, by area?

632. Name 2 caves with ancient wall paintings, one in Spain, the other in France.

633. In the 6th century, a Byzantine emperor built 3 churches, each one a precious art monument: San Vitale in Ravenna, Italy; Santa Sofia in Istanbul, Turkey; name the third church, the area, and the country.

634. The unit of currenty in Kuwait is a *dinar*. It can be divided into 1000 what?

635. In Scotland, New Year's Eve is a holiday. What is it called?

636. What capital city is served by Faaa International Airport?

637. There are many stone monuments on which remote island dependency of Chile?

638. A hard liquor of reddish color, with a worm inside the bottle, is available in Mexico. What is it called?

639. Name the main shopping street in New York City.

640. Which is the oldest university town in Europe?

631. U.S.S.R.
632. Altamira, Spain; Lescaux, France
633. St. Catherine, Sinai, Egypt
634. *Fils*
635. *Hogmanay*
636. Papeete, Tahiti
637. Easter Island
638. *Mezcal*
639. Fifth Avenue
640. Bologna, Italy

QUESTIONS...

641. If you wanted to see the entire Smoky Mountain chain, which 3 American states would you cross?

642. Which country is best known for its fondues?

643. Which shop on London's Picadilly might tempt you with a wide variety of gourmet foods?

644. In what country will you find Djenne and Gao, towns on the trans-Sahara caravan route?

645. Which was the first island discovered by Columbus in the western hemisphere?

646. What is a Turkish bath called in Turkey?

647. Which god is venerated in Angkor Wat, Kampuchea?

648. Name a city founded by Greeks, named by Gauls, built by Romans and medieval Christians, and painted by Van Gogh.

649. Ajanta and Ellora, India's famous painted caves, are to be found in the same state. Name it.

650. What U.S. city has a voodoo museum?

...ANSWERS

641. Georgia, North Carolina, Tennessee
642. Switzerland
643. Fortnum and Mason
644. Mali
645. San Salvador Island (Bahamas)
646. *Hammam*
647. Visnu
648. Arles, France
649. Maharastra
650. New Orleans, Louisiana

651. When you see *Hagenbuttensuppe* on a German menu, what kind of soup are you being offered?

652. Name the northernmost and southernmost American states connected by the Appalachian trail.

653. In what city can you see a shield commemorating the birth of Catherine the Great, empress of Russia?

654. What country occupies the largest archipelago in the world?

655. Name an ancient city, now a seaharbor town in Kenya.

656. Which are the 3 U.S. Virgin Islands?

657. What is known in Scandinavian countries as *sauna* is also an old Russian tradition. What is it called there?

658. Name a university town on the Volga that was once capital of the Tartar empire.

659. Whose airline is AMI?

660. The temple of Aphrodite in the town of Kouklia was a pilgrimage center of ancient Greece. Where is it located?

651. Rosehip
652. Maine, Georgia
653. Szczecin, Poland
654. Indonesia
655. Mombasa
656. St. Thomas, St. Croix, St. John
657. *Banya*
658. Kazan, U.S.S.R.
659. Marshall Islands
660. Cyprus

661. Voodoo is a ceremony performed on which of the Caribbean islands?

662. Soda bread is a specialty of which country?

663. Which is the only American state divided into parishes instead of counties?

664. Where in the Sahara were primitive Stone Age paintings discovered?

665. What is the second largest island in the world?

666. In what Japanese city is Daitokuji, the zen Temple of Great Virtue?

667. Gilbert and Ellice Islands, formerly a British colony, now form which republic?

668. Thousands of Hindu pilgrims immerse themselves in the waters of the river Ganges in which central Indian city?

669. What Pacific islands are famous for their stone money?

670. What is the Argentine cowboy called?

661. Haiti
662. Ireland
663. Louisiana
664. Tassili mountains, Algeria
665. New Guinea
666. Kyoto
667. Kiribati
668. Varanasi (Benares)
669. Yap Islands
670. *Gaucho*

671. What kind of cheese is used in Greek salads?

672. In which archipelago are New Britain and New Ireland the 2 largest islands?

673. From where in the United States did the first airplane take off?

674. Which is the tallest art deco building in the world?

675. Jujuy is a picturesque town once favored by the Incas for its hot water springs. In which country is it located?

676. The Castle of Vaduz is the home of a reigning monarch. What country is it in?

677. What is the biggest seaport, and second largest city in Japan?

678. On what Caribbean island can you watch the local dance, the *tumba*?

679. What was the home of the largest trout in the world?

680. The spoken language of this country is *Sranang Tongo*, popularly known as *Taki-Taki*; the official language is Dutch. Name the country.

671. *Feta*
672. Bismark Archipelago, Pacific Islands
673. Kill Devil Hill, Kitty hawk, North Carolina
674. Empire State Building, New York City
675. Argentina
676. Liechtenstein
677. Yokohama
678. Curacao (north West Indies)
679. Pend Oreille, Idaho
680. Surinam (northeast South America)

681. Name the Italian speaking section of Switzerland.

682. In what city will you find Castillo de San Marcos, the oldest masonry fort in the United States?

683. Nan Madol, a city dating from the 12th century but now abandoned, is called the "Venice of the Pacific." What island is it on?

684. What food is called *Delice de Saint-Cyr*, in France?

685. What is the driest place in the world, where you can see designs made in the desert sands hundreds of years ago?

686. What country offers you the most performances by flamenco dancers?

687. An Italian thruway called Autostrada della Sanenissima runs between 2 cities whose names begin with the letter "t". Name them.

688. Copan, the ruins of the first Mayan capital, are regarded as one of the most beautiful archaeological sights in the world. In which country can you admire them?

689. Name the wall built in the north of England by a Roman emperor.

690. Bandar Seri Begawan is the capital of what Asian country?

681. Ticino
682. St. Augustine, Florida
683. Ponape, Caroline Islands
684. A kind of cheese
685. Nazra, Peru
686. Spain
687. Trieste and Torino
688. Honduras
689. Hadrian's Wall
690. Brunei

691. The Arawak Indians were the original population of a Caribbean island. Where can you see the largest collection of their relics?

692. Jason is said to have started his journey with the Argonauts from a city now in Yugoslavia. Which one?

693. In which city can you visit a museum containing the Aegina marbles, a collection of statues from the island of Aegina?

694. The gothic Harkness Tower is a dominant landmark well worth a visit. In which eastern U.S. university does it stand?

695. Name the North Atlantic country whose capital is Torshavn.

696. The Egyptian Obelisk is the largest in the world. Where can it be seen?

697. Which national capital is situated at the greatest height?

698. Name a Caribbean island shared by the French and the Dutch.

699. What country, with less than 10,000 citizens, has no capital city?

700. In 2 B.C. there were 7 wonders of the world. Five have now been destroyed without trace. Name the remaining 2, and where you can see them.

691. Port de Paix, Tortuga Island, Haiti

692. Ljubljana

693. Munich, West Germany (Glyptotheke)

694. Yale University, Connecticut

695. Faroe Islands

696. Hippodrome, Istanbul, Turkey

697. La Paz, Bolivia

698. St. Martin/Sint Maarten

699. Nauru in the Pacific Ocean

700.Pyramids of Giza, Egypt; Temple of Artemis of the Ephesians, Ephesus, Turkey

QUESTIONS...

701. Name the island group which includes Anegada, Jost Van Dyke and Virgin Gorda.

702. In what country is the principal resort city named La Libertad?

703. One of the finest collections of impressionist art can be seen by appointment only. Name the museum, and the metropolitan area of the U.S.A. in which it is located.

704. Which people speak the Slavic language in the middle of Germany?

705. There are 5 oceans–the Pacific, the Atlantic, the Indian -name the other 2.

706. In what country is *baeri* the name for a milkbar?

707. Aphrodisias, an ancient art center, supplied Imperial Rome with sculptures. In what country can you see the ruins of the city?

708. In what country can you order *Geheck*, a soup made of pork, veal lungs and plums?

709. If you vacation on the Azores, and wish to go to every island, how many would you visit?

710. Which French city is famous for its Gothic cathedral, described by Henry James as "a sort of tapering bouquet of sculptured stone"?

701. British Virgin Islands
702. El Salvador
703. Barnes Collection, Philadelphia, Pennsylvania
704. Wenden
705. The Arctic, the Antarctic
706. Finland
707. Turkey
708. Luxembourg
709. Nine
710. Chartres

QUESTIONS...

711. Which American state has the motto, *Esse Quam Viderai* (to be rather than to seem)?

712. The German city of Koenigsberg is now part of the U.S.S.R. What has it been renamed?

713. The Roman emperor, Hadrian, built himself a villa that was a marvel of architectural achievement. Where can you see its ruins?

714. In what country are trucks or carts selling sausages and beer called *polsevogne*?

715. Jerez de la Frontera, a historic Spanish town, produces one of the most popular wines in the world. Name it.

716. What is the difference between the Russian and Polish toasts, "to your health!"?

717. What English cathedral was the scene of the world's most famous murder?

718. What dance is Vienna best known for?

719. In what country can you buy *snakak*, a bread measuring 24 by 10 inches?

720. In what part of France is the Cote d'Or?

711. North Carolina

712. Kaliningrad

713. Tivoli, Italy

714. Denmark

715. Sherry

716. The letter "o" (Russian-*na zdorovie*; Polish–*na zdrovie*)

717. Canterbury (Thomas a Beckett died)

718. Waltz

719. Iran

720. Burgundy

721. On which London square is the National Gallery?

722. In which state in the U.S.A. is key lime pie a specialty?

723. In what country is a tavern called a *mahna*?

724. From what is *Calvados*, a liquor distilled in Normandy, made?

725. What was Poland's first capital?

726. Name the small swift boat which plies the river Nile.

727. What is the country that lies at the heart of Africa?

728. Which mountain chain divides Europe from Africa?

729. The song, *"Torna, torna..."* refers to which Italian city?

730. Mocha, once a great coffee port, is in what country?

...ANSWERS

721. Trafalgar
722. Florida
723. Bulgaria
724. Apples
725. Gniezno
726. *Felucca*
727. Central African Republic
728. Urals
729. Sorrento
730. Yemen Arab Republic

731. Name the only country on the South American continent in which English is the national language.

732. Somerset bridge is the smallest drawbridge in the world. Lifting the 18-inch plank permits the passage of sailboats. Where is it?

733. What Caribbean island passed between British and French hands 14 times?

734. One of the best collections of Russian art outside the U.S.S.R. can be seen in the United States, by appointment only. Name the museum and the city.

735. Two European islands gave their names to American states. Name the islands.

736. What 2 things do Kingman Reef, Navassa and Palmyra islands have in common?

737. A Glaswegian is an inhabitant of what city?

738. In what country is the meat dish, *Hoppel-Poppel*, a specialty?

739. In El Paso, Texas, what is the fence dividing the United States and Mexico called?

740. In London it is called the underground, in New York, the subway. What is it called in Washington, D.C.?

731. Guyana

732. Bermuda

733. St. Lucia

734. Merriweather Post Museum, Washington, D.C.

735. Rhodes, Greece; Jersey, Channel Islands, U.K.

736. All outlying territories of the U.S.; all uninhabited

737. Glasgow, Scotland

738. Germany

739. Tortilla Curtain

740. Metro

741. Name the fermented mare's milk, drunk by many nomadic Steppe peoples.

742. What kind of food are *Mont des Cats* and *Mont d'Or*?

743. What country is referred to as the Switzerland of Central America?

744. In what city can you visit the restored acropolis of Pergammon, in the Pergammon Museum?

745. *Yerba mate* is the national drink of what country?

746. What is the present name of the island group once known as the Malvinas?

747. Leningrad lies on what river?

748. What is the country formerly known as British and French New Hebrides, and famous for its primitive art?

749. Where is Mexican Hat, a Navajo Indian trading post?

750. Which is the main island of Fiji?

741. *Kumys*
742. French cheeses
743. Costa Rica
744. Berlin
745. Uruguay
746. Falkland Islands
747. Neva
748. Repulic of Vanuatu
749. Utah
750. Vitu Levu

751. What is the monetary unit of Western Samoa?

752. In the 18th century a trip to Paris or Rome was *de rigeur* for a gentleman. What was such a journey called?

753. What is the name of Sumer's holy city, the religious center of the world's oldest civilization. In what country can you see its ruins?

754. What islands, formerly called 11,000 Virgines, are the only dependency of France in North America?

755. Which American state was named after a mythical island in a medieval Spanish romance?

756. What well-preserved English medieval town was attacked by French forces from Honfleur in the 16th century, and is now twinned with that city?

757. Name a republic within a group of islands in the Atlantic Ocean, with Portuguese as its official language.

758. Two Caribbean capitals are Kingston and Kingstown. Name their countries.

759. Name 2 counties named after famous explorers.

760. In what country are you if you hear Divehi spoken around you?

751. *Tala*
752. Grand Tour
753. Nippur, Iraq
754. St. Pierre and Miquelon
755. California
756. Sandwich
757. Cape Verde
758. Jamaica, St. Vincent
759. Colombia, Cook Islands
760. Maldive Islands

761. What is the capital in the west Pacific whose capital is Nuku'alofa?

762. In what town can you attend Duke University?

763. Name the baroque palace of the Duke of Marlborough.

764. Giselbertus created Romanesque sculptures for a church. Where can you see it?

765. Three American states were named after 2 English kings. Name the kings and the states.

766. Sans Souci castle was built for Frederick the Great in Germany. A famous castle of the same name was built on a Caribbean island. In which country?

767. What is the monetary unit of the kingdom of Lesotho?

768. What is the federal Islamic republic with Moroni as its capital?

769. It is called *shish-kabob* in the Near East, and *shashlik* in the U.S.S.R. What is this meat dish called in Greece?

770. What capital city has the smallest population in both the continental Americas?

761. Tonga

762. Durham, North Carolina, U.S.A.

763. Blenheim

764. Autun, France (St. Lazare)

765. King Charles I: North and South Carolina;
King George II: Georgia

766. Haiti

767. *Loti*

768. Comoros

769. *Souvlaki*

770. Belmopan, Belize (c. 3,000)

QUESTIONS...

771. Which American state was named after a French king?

772. What has been added to McDonald's "Big Mac" in German-speaking countries?

773. Where is Ugarit, the ancient city where tablets written in the oldest alphabet were found?

774. Where can you see a statue of Alexander Selkirk, the model for Defoe's Robinson Crusoe?

775. Catal Huyuk is thought to be one of the oldest towns in existence. In what modern country is it located?

776. The fountain of youth is said to be in a rain forest on Puerto Rico. Name it.

777. What castle do archaeologists now think could have been Camelot?

778. In what city does Frederick II's Cuba Castle now stand in the center of a park?

779. In what American state is Sequoia National Park, with the largest trees in the world?

780. On what river do the grapes for the wine *Chateau Neuf du Pape* grow?

771. Louisiana
772. The letter "k" (Big Mack)
773. Syria
774. Largo, Scotland
775. Turkey
776. El Yunque
777. Cadbury Castle
778. Palermo, Sicily
779. California
780. Rhone

781. In what country is *kasseri* one of the most popular cheeses?

782. If you wish to take a French road equivalent to a turnpike or thruway in the U.S.A., what do you ask for?

783. If you wish to take an English road equivalent to a turnpike or thruway in the U.S.A., what do you ask for?

784. In which American city is there a French Quarter?

785. The alps are shared by 7 European countries. Name them.

786. One of the oldest kingdoms in the world, Dilmun, was on an island. What is its modern name?

787. If you want to search for Brazilian emerald (green tourmaline) on a visit to the U.S.A., to which state must you go?

788. Where did Monet, the French impressionist, spend his last years painting his garden?

789. Templar's Castle is in which Portuguese city?

790. What is the best preserved city remaining from Roman antiquity? In what country is it?

781. Greece

782. *Autoroute*

783. Motorway

784. New Orleans, Louisiana

785. Albania, Austria, France, Germany, Italy, Switzerland, Yugoslavia

786. Bahrein

787. California

788. Giverny, France

789. Tomar

790. Leptis Magna, Libya

791. What famous house appears on the five-cent U.S. coin, and where is it located?

792. Name the city in which the festival *Palio* has taken place twice a year in Piazza del Campo, since the 13th century.

793. On what island will you find Dunvegan Castle, where Dr. Johnson and Boswell once spent a week?

794. The Olmec people, who preceded the Mayans and Aztecs, lived on which isthmus?

795. The best preserved ancient Greek wall paintings are in a town originally called Poseidonia. What is its current name, and in which country is it?

796. In what city can you see the Well of Moses, with sculptures by Claus Sluter?

797. Hopping between Scottish islands, you encounter names with the Gaelic *bail*, or Old Norse *wick*. What do these mean in English?

798. What are the fastest trains in Germany?

799. In what country can you visit the Kashub Switzerland?

800. Name Frederick II's castle in Apulia.

...ANSWERS

791. Monticello, Virgina
792. Siena, Italy
793. Skye, Scotland
794. Techuantepec
795. Paestum, Italy
796. Dijon, France
797. Village
798. Inter-city
799. Poland
800. Castel del Monte

801. Hymetus honey, considered the best in the world, comes from which country?

802. What is the first Mexican city you will encounter south of San Diego?

803. Name the fastest train between Washington, D.C. and New York.

804. What lake is pictured on a German bill that circulated as currency before 1947?

805. In Chinese lettering, one symbol represents a pig, another, a roof. When the 2 are combined, with the pig under the roof, what does it mean?

806. What is the Silk Road's easternmost point?

807. Name the country formerly called East Pakistan.

808. Two Italian towns give their names to the words "milliner" and "pistol". Name them.

809. The Sultanate of Brunei is located on which island?

810. A, AL and AND designate cars from which countries?

...ANSWERS

801. Greece
802. Tijuana
803. Metroliner
804. Koenigsee, Bavaria
805. Happiness
806. The Syrian coast
807. Bangladesh
808. Milan, Pitoia
809. Borneo
810. Austria, Albania, Andorra

811. Name the city built by Alexander the Great in 331 B.C., and the country it is in.

812. What do Germans call their thruways?

813. Which country has the largest airport?

814. Name the walled town that is one of Portugal's showpieces.

815. What Indian Ocean island, made famous by an error in its stamp of 1847, is now an independent country?

816. In what country live both the smallest monkeys, the tarsius, and some of the biggest eagles, called monkeyeaters?

817. In what city can you shop on Temple Street, one of the world's busiest streets, with stores open 24 hours?

818. On what Caribbean island are the fashionable beach resorts, Montego Bay and Ocho Rios?

819. Connaught Place is the center of which city?

820. To the Paguan tribes, the ideal of female beauty is a long neck, so girls wear neck rings weighing over 20 pounds, from childhood. Name the Paguans' country.

811. Alexandria, Egypt

812. *Autobahnen*

813. Saudi Arabia

814. Obidos

815. Mauritius

816. Philippines

817. Hong Kong

818. Jamaica

819. New Delhi, India

820. Myanmar (Burma)

QUESTIONS...

821. In what country is it the custom for a man to kiss a woman's hand along with a handshake?

822. *Laaka*, a cloudberry liquor, is the specialty of what country?

823. The Tuesday after Whitsunday is "Jumping Procession Day". For the last 500 years, the citizens of what city have jumped around their cathedral on that day?

824. Which country's capital is on the river Spree?

825. Name the German town from which the Pied Piper set out.

826. Alba, a town in Piedmont, Italy, is said to grow the most delectable mushrooms. Name them.

827. The Swiss *franc* is a national monetary unit. In the French and Italian sections of the country it can be divided into 100 *centimes*; in the German section it equals 100 what?

828. What is the name of Berlin's famous avenue lined with tupelo trees?

829. In what city can you see the house in which the painter Esteban Murillo died?

830. In what city can you visit a museum with Queen Mathilda's tapestry of 1077, depicting the Normans' recent conquest of England?

821. Poland
822. Finland
823. Echternach, Luxembourg
824. Germany (Berlin)
825. Hameln
826. White truffles
827. *Rappen*
828. Unter den Linden
829. Seville, Spain
830. Bayeux, France

QUESTIONS...

831. *Waterzoi*, stewed chicken in broth with cream and eggs, is the specialty of what country?

832. Who was the American writer who described Rhine wine as vinegar under a different label and edelweiss as a flower the color of bad cigar ash?

833. What is a mix of cabbage and potatoes called in Ireland?

834. Name the great museum of Frankfurt, Germany.

835. In Greek legend the winged horse Pegasus kicked a mountain, where sprang forth a fountain called *hipppocrene*. Muses came to drink its waters for inspiration. Name the mountain.

836. Little remains of Emperor Nero's palace; it was destroyed except for a few rooms which were incorporated into what?

837. Where can you see the tallest full-figure statue, and what is its name?

838. For night entertainment, "Crazy Horse" is one of the most famous spots in the world. Where is it located?

839. Alcohol stored in an oak barrel for 20 years is cherished as a special drink in Poland. What is it called?

840. What do Mexicans call the musicians who perform at their weddings?

831. Belgium
832. Mark Twain
833. *Colcannon*
834. Staedliches Museum
835. Mount Helicon
836. Trajan baths
837. Volgograd, U.S.S.R; *Motherland*
838. Paris, France
839. *Starka*
840. *Mariachi*

841. According to an ancient Chinese saying, "There is paradise in heaven and on earth" in these 2 cities. Name them.

842. What large painting used to hang in a duke's bedroom and can now be seen one third in the Uffizi Museum in Florence, one third in the Louvre, in Paris, and one third in the National Gallery in London?

843. A drink made out of raspberries is called *framboise* in France. What is it called in Germany?

844. Pole cats can be found in 3 European countries. Which ones?

845. In what city can you see the equestrian statue of *condottiere Colleoni* by Andrea Verocchio?

846. Which wine is made in the Basque province of Spain?

847. Which town in the Netherlands has an ancient house which bears an inscription stating that Erasmus was conceived there and born in Rotterdam?

848. Where is U.S. president Franklin D. Roosevelt's house and museum?

849. Only one woman out of thousands refused Casanova's advances. Name the street and the town where this happened.

850. A popular style of music called "highlife" is special to which African country?

841. Hangzhou, Suzhou
842. *Rout of San Romano* by Uccello
843. *Himbeergeist*
844. Soviet Union, Romania, Bulgaria
845. Venice, Italy
846. *Chacoli*
847. Gouda
848. Hyde Park, New York
849. Denmark Street, Soho, London
850. Ghana

QUESTIONS...

851. Things that float on the sea from a ship's wreckage are called flotsam. What are things that float because they were thrown out to lighten the load?

852. What is the Scottish national dish of sheep's entrails, oats and other ingredients sewn up in a sheep's stomach?

853. What capital has the Temple of Heavenly Peace as a landmark?

854. A water taxi is the best way to get around Srinagar, Kashmir. What is it called?

855. The ruins of what temple begun twenty centuries ago can be seen in Ur, Iraq?

856. What are the following: Washington, Lafayette, Hood, and Kosciusko?

857. In what city is the cathedral of St. Sernin?

858. Two European cities are crisscrossed by canals, creating numerous islands. Venice has 90 islands; which is the other city, with over 100?

859. Which is the "Eternal City"?

860. What German city was known as Braustadt (Brewery City) hundreds of years ago?

851. Jestam
852. *Haggis*
853. Beijing (Peking), China
854. *Shikara*
855. Ziggurat
856. Mountains
857. Toulouse, France
858. Amsterdam, The Netherlands
859. Rome, Italy
860. Hamburg

861. What are the following: St. Florent, St. Malo, St. Eufemia, and Riga?

862. Guadeloupe, the Caribbean island, is shaped like a butterfly–2 islands connected by a drawbridge. Name each of these islands.

863. From what Swiss city does gin derive its name?

864. There is a Van Gogh museum in Amsterdam. Another important collection of his works is in what park in the Netherlands?

865. The Welsh castles of Beaumaris, Caernarvon and Conway were all built in the reign of which English king?

866. *Yuan*, the Chinese monetary unit, can be divided into 10 what?

867. When you have a shamrock stamped into your passport, what island are you entering?

868. What region of Greece has almost inaccessible 14th-century monasteries built on top of rock columns?

869. "Fragments of Eden" is the poetic name of the only granite island chain in the world. Name it.

870. If you stop for a street treat of *falafel*, where are you likely to be?

...ANSWERS

861. Inlets
862. Basse Terre, Grand Terre
863. Geneva
864. Hooge Veluwe National Park
865. Edward I
866. *Jiao*
867. Montserrat, British West Indies
868. Meteora
869. Seychelles
870. Israel

871. Name the famous beer hall in Munich.

872. An American book published in 1825 described the natives of which country as "of good stature, and inclined to be corpulent, but remarkable in general for heavy awkward mien with regular features, and fair complexion"?

873. The 15 highest mountains in Europe are all in one country. Name it.

874. Basseterre and Basse-Terre are the capitals of which 2 Caribbean islands?

875. In what city can you admire the equestrian statue of *condottiere Gatta Melatta* by Donatello?

876. The Romans built a city for their soldiers in what is now Spain, and called it Augusta Emerita. What is it called today?

877. The former capital of Hungary is no longer part of that country. Name the city.

878. Name the rail pass valid for unlimited travel in India.

879. Marc Anthony was sailing a ship off what coast when he decided to abandon his fleet to join Cleopatra?

880. In Oman, the unit of currency is the *rial*. It can be divided into 1,000 what?

871. Hofbrauhaus
872. The Netherlands
873. U.S.S.R.
874. St. Christopher-Nevis, Guadeloupe
875. Padua, Italy
876. Merida
877. Bratislava (formerly Poczony)
878. Indrail pass
879. Western Greece
880. *Biazas*

881. In what city can you see the excellent collection of Rubens paintings in the Ringling Museum of Art?

882. On what plain, in which country is the monument Stonehenge located?

883. Canaletto, an 18th-century Italian painter, is famous for his panoramas of Venice and London. He also painted which eastern European capital?

884. In which southern French city is one of the most important film festivals held annually?

885. The museum Meyer van der Bergh is located in what city?

886. Most of this country, which abolished slavery in 1980, lies in the Sahara desert. Name it.

887. Eastern Malaysia occupies northern Borneo. What are the names of the 2 states there?

888. The area north of the French city of Bordeaux produces a world famous brandy called *cognac*. What is the name of the brandy produced south of the city?

889. When traveling in north Africa you will be aware of a wind blowing from the south. What is it called?

890. Name 2 independent European countries located on islands, each with a population of less than half a million.

...ANSWERS

881. Sarasota, Florida
882. Salisbury Plain, England
883. Warsaw, Poland
884. Cannes
885. Antwerp, Belgium
886. Mauritania
887. Sarawak, Sabah
888. *Armagnac*
889. *Sirocco*
890. Malta, Iceland

QUESTIONS...

891. Which U.S. town started a dance craze in the 1920s?

892. American Indians used to built temporary abodes from sticks and branches. What is the name of such a dwelling?

893. Which Scottish island has 8 breweries of malt whisky?

894. Which country must pay a Spanish bishop annual tribute of 460 *pesetas*, 6 hams, 12 capons and 26 slates of cheese?

895. Where can you see a group of houses called *Fuggerei*, built four and a half centuries ago?

896. On what 2 Pacific islands are the descendants of the mutineers of the *Bounty* still the majority of the population?

897. Where is the Bradford Brinton Memorial Ranch Museum located?

898. What is the word often used by the Malayan people meaning to wander or travel?

899. In what Italian city is *Maggio Musicale* (musical May) celebrated?

900. Pea soup with meat and sausages, called *Ertwen*, is one of the most popular dishes in what country?

891. Charleston, South Carolina
892. *Ramada*
893. Islay
894. Andorra
895. Augsburg, Germany
896. Norfolk, Pitcairn
897. Horn, Wyoming, U.S.A.
898. *Jalan-jalan*
899. Florence
900. The Netherlands

901. What is an island consisting of a coral reef surrounding a lagoon called?

902. How many humps does a Bactrian camel have?

903. The dodo, a bird now extinct, used to live on what 2 islands in the Indian Ocean?

904. The Italian specialy, rugola salad, is made with what kind of greens?

905. What country can you reach by sailing either on the Caspian Sea or the Persian Gulf?

906. Name the stately processional dance which originated in Poland.

907. The Beagle Channel, named after Darwin's ship, washes the southern shores of what island?

908. What people wear a woolen cap called a *glengarry*?

909. Both Mexico and the island of Jamaica produce excellent coffee liqueurs. Name them.

910. What city was founded by the Spaniards in 1610 on the site of an old Indian pueblo, and is the oldest seat of a state government in the U.S.A. today?

...ANSWERS

901. Atol
902. Two
903. La Reunion, Mauritius
904. Dandelion leaves
905. Iran
906. Polonaise
907. Tierra del Fuego
908. Scots
909. Kahlua, Tia Maria
910. Santa Fe, New Mexico

QUESTIONS...

911. Name the brimless hat, shaped like a truncated cone, worn in the eastern Mediterranean.

912. On what mountain are the grapes for the wine *Lacrima Christi* grown?

913. What are Eskimo dwellings made of blocks of ice called?

914. According to Greek legend, what monster has a lion's body, a woman's head, and eats anyone who cannot answer its questions?

915. Name the small South American fish which attacks and devours animals.

916. Name the fast-running Australian bird related to the ostrich.

917. Name the best known blue-veined cheeses of France and Italy.

918. In what American city can you watch the exciting 500-mile car race on Memorial Day?

919. In what country do they celebrate *Ekpe-Ekpe*, a fesival when bonfires are lit on each street corner so the dead may light their pipes?

920. Two African countries have capitals with names meaning the same, one in English, one in French. Name the capitals and their countries.

911. Fez

912. Mt. Vesuvius

913. Igloos

914. Sphinx

915. Piranha

916. Emu

917. Roquefort, Gorgonzola

918. Indianapolis, Indiana

919. Togo

920. Freetown, Sierra Leone; Libreville, Gabon

921. Identify these 3 types of African antelope:

(a) with horns curving down

(b) with horns curving in a spiral

(c) with straight horns

922. Name the Californian mission which was planned midway between San Diego and San Gabriel.

923. Name the special Italian custard made with Marsala wine, and the Spanish variety made with caramel.

924. What are the warders of the Tower of London called?

925. Punto Arenas is the southernmost city of which continent?

926. In what city can you see paintings at the Courtauld Gallery?

927. What is the name of the Alpine-like village in Haiti?

928. Where in Germany can you visit the grave of Charlotte Kestner, the "Lotte" in Goethe's *Werther*?

929. *Mongorokom* is a white liquid extracted from a mixture of manioc and maize in which country?

930. To what island was Seneca exiled after he seduced Tulia, a student who was the niece of Emperor Claudius?

921. (a) Gnu; (b) eland; (c) onyx
922. San Juan Capistrano
923. *Zabaglione; flan*
924. Beefeaters
925. South America
926. London, England
927. Kenscoff
928. Hanover, Germany
929. Gabon
930. Corsica

QUESTIONS...

931. In what country is *foutou*, a ball of paste made from yams, cassava or bananas, and dipped in palmgrain oil, the specialty?

932. What is the controversial museum, built in the 1970s in Paris and named after a French president, called?

933. On what Italian island did Napoleon spend his first exile?

934. Name a country where the chief industry is beer-making.

935. The name Massachusetts is derived from the American Indian phrase, *"massa dchu es at."* What does it mean?

936. Where can you see the ruins of the Bronze Age Cucuruzza fortress?

937. Because students in this German town dueled too often with officers stationed there, the university moved to Munich. Name the town.

938. What Russian town was a medieval republic, and a member of the Hanseatic league?

939. In what African country will you find the source of the river Nile?

940. Name the hard liquor produced by the Icelandic government, sold in a bottle with a black label.

931. Ivory Coast
932. Centre Pompidou
933. Elba
934. Cameroon
935. Great hill, small place
936. Corsica
937. Ingolstadt
938. Novgorod
939. Uganda
940. *Potvin*

941. What 2 countries with names beginning with "c" have both French and English as their official languages?

942. After which queen was the American state of Maryland named?

943. If you are eating *enchiladas*, *tacos* and *tortillas* in their country of origin, where are you traveling?

944. What are the 2 official languages of Czechoslovakia?

945. Where can you drink *koutoukou*-a palm wine with "a thoroughly established treacherous reputation"?

946. What are the following: Austerlitz, Jena, Sebastopol, Louvre?

947. What kind of transport is San Fransisco famed for?

948. The 3 major cities of what country are Ouagadougou, Bobo-Dioulasso and Koudougou?

949. What is the monetary unit of Ethiopia?

950. The life expectancy in Norway, Iceland, and Switzerland is about 75 years. What is it for the people of Gabon?

...ANSWERS

941. Canada, Cameroon
942. Henrietta Maria, wife of Britain's Charles I
943. Mexico
944. Slovak, Czech
945. Ivory Coast
946. Paris metro stations
947. Cablecars
948. Burkina Faso
949. *Birr*
950. 33 years

QUESTIONS...

951. If you wish to buy the French pastry known in the U.S.A. as a Napoleon, what would you ask for in France?

952. Where are the CIA offices, the center of U.S. intelligence, located?

953. Where was the biggest tank battle in world history fought?

954. What is the highest structure in the U.S.A.?

955. What is the most densely populated country in Europe?

956. In Bombay, India, what is the name of the small paddle boat?

957. In 1883 a train route was inaugurated providing luxury service between Paris and Istanbul. What was it called?

958. What kind of person likes to collect picture postcards?

959. While visiting what metropolis can you see Paul Landowski's statue of Christ on top of a mountain?

960. What Mexican city lies directly south of El Paso, Texas?

951. *Mille feuilles*
952. Langley, Virginia
953. Kursk, U.S.S.R.
954. Gateway Arc, St. Louis, Missouri
955. Monaco
956. Dingey
957. Orient Express
958. Deltiologist
959. Rio de Janeiro, Brazil
960. Juarez

961. Catherine the Great, empress of Russia, built a palace in Pushkin. What was the village called before the revolution?

962. Name the cold vegetable soup seasoned with vinegar and oil, a specialty of Spain and Latin America.

963. What is the official language of Ethiopia?

964. Which U.S. state derives its name from the Spanish word meaning "big-eared men"?

965. What king built Neuschwanstein, one of the most photographed castles in the world?

966. Name the fortress in Israel where the Zealots, rather than surrendering to the Romans, committed suicide.

967. Name the London street known as the center of newspapers and journalism.

968. The trademark "4711" is one of the most advertised in Germany. Name the product and the city in which it is made.

969. What sea separates Italy and Yugoslavia?

970. Bagpipes are played by Polish mountaineers, but what do they call the instrument?

...ANSWERS

961. Tsarskoe Selo
962. *Gazpacho*
963. Amharic
964. Oregon (*orejon*)
965. Ludwig II of Bavaria
966. Masada
967. Fleet Street
968. Cologne, Cologne
969. Adriatic Sea
970. *Kobza*

971. Northern and Southern Rhodesia are two former British colonies whose names now begin with 'z'. What are they?

972. If you wish to buy a long, narrow loaf of bread in France, what should you ask for?

973. What is the architectural term for an arch extending from a wall to a supporting abutment, used in Gothic cathedrals?

974. On what street in which city is the financial center of the U.S.A.?

975. What is the name for a large merchant ship with a rich cargo?

976. White and green signs with the outline of a crowned Roman goblet mark a scenic route along the river Rhine. What is the name of the road?

977. Where are the offices of the British prime minister located?

978. Name the Italian specialty dish from Umbria-spaghetti with wild asparagus, eggs and bacon.

979. What is the official language of the African country, Lesotho?

980. What is the monetary unit of Ghana?

971. Zambia, Zimbabwe
972. *Baguette*
973. Flying buttress
974. Wall Street, New York
975. Argosy
976. Rheingau Riesling route
977. 10 Downing Street, London
978. *Alla boscaiola*
979. Lesotho
980. *Cedi*

981. A left-handed dictionary defines a favorite place for honeymooners in the U.S.A. as "marriage on the rocks" or "the second disapppointment in marriage". What does it refer to?

982. Name a favorite German dish, a soup made with beans and meat and served as a complete meal.

983. Near what French town did the first tank battle take place?

984. What country claims to have discovered the legendary Land of Ophir where King Solomon's gold was mined?

985. Where can you see the ill-fated London Bridge?

986. A European country derives most of its legitimate income from an activity prohibited to its own citizens. Name the activity and the country.

987. Malmsey wine, also called *malvoisie*, can be found everywhere on the island where it is produced. Name the island.

988. Where can you visit the house where Rudyard Kipling was born?

989. The Florian Gate is a landmark of what Polish city?

990. What nomadic people inhabits parts of the Sahara and still practises slavery?

...ANSWERS

981. Niagara Falls
982. *Eintopf*
983. Cambrai, France
984. Zimbabwe
985. Lake Havasu City, Arizona, U.S.A.
986. Gambling, Monaco
987. Corsica
988. Bombay, India
989. Krakow
990. *Tuareg*

QUESTIONS...

991. An American stamp issued in the 1980s commemorates the Friendship Bridge between which 2 countries?

992. Name the traditional attire of Scotsmen.

993. What is the name of the German wine made from pressed and frozen grapes?

994. Where is it said that Adam and Eve met after their expulsion form paradise?

995. What is the name for a four-wheeled carriage drawn by horses in eastern European Slavic countries?

996. Name the oldest castle in the world–it has 20 stories and was built in 100 A.D.

997. Rome is built on 7 hills on either side of which river?

998. The Chinese try to achieve excellence in 3 aspects of food preparation: taste is one, name the other two.

999. In what African country did Alex Haley, author of *Roots*, search for his ancestors?

1000. Where in Switzerland can you visit the Peace Palace?

...ANSWERS

991. Canada and U.S.A.
992. Kilt
993. *Eiswein*
994. Mount Ararat
995. *Droshky*
996. Gomadan, Yemen
997. Tiber
998. Appearance, aroma
999. Gambia
1000. Geneva

1001. "A lyric poem in stone, flowing round the crown of a hill to the musical accompaniment of a jagged mountain range...and a green expanse of rice fields." Which Javan Buddhist temple was Arnold Toynbee describing?

1002. Mexico and Egypt are famous for their ancient pyramids. In which European metropolis will you find a modern one?

1003. "Where idleness ranks among the virtues," wrote Oscar Wilde of one of the richest communities on the north east coast of America. Name it.

1004. Cheddar, Gruyere and Roquefort are cheeses named after the towns in which they are produced. In which 3 countries are these towns located?

1005. How many languages are spoken in the Balkan peninsula? Name them.

1006. How many countries does the equator pass through on the Asian continent?

1007. *Dobra* is a feminine adjective meaning "good" in Polish. There are 2 towns of this name in Poland, one in Yugoslavia, and yet 2 more in which other country?

1008. Bengali is spoken in East Bengal, India. It is also the official language of which country?

1009. French Indochina comprised 3 countries: Vietnam, Kampuchea, and...?

1010. Name the city whose rose-red ruins are the most celebrated in Jordan.

1001. Borobudur

1002. Paris

1003. Newport, Rhode Island

1004. Great Britain, Switzerland, France

1005. 6: Albanian, Bulgarian, Greek, Macedonian, Serbo-Croatian, Slovene

1006. None

1007. Romania

1008. Bangladesh

1009. Laos

1010. Petra

QUESTIONS...

1011. Which American island did Jan Morris describe as a "haven for the ambitious"?

1012. What is the popular alcoholic beverage of Japan?

1013. What yoghurt drink is popular in India?

1014. In which Latin American country will you see Indian women wearing Homburg hats?

1015. Name the capital situated on the river Tigrus.

1016. Two languages are spoken in Sri Lanka: Tamil and...?

1017. The French Chateau de Malmaison is now home to a Napoleonic museum. Which famous woman called it home from 1799 to 1814?

1018. Galicia, in northwestern Spain, has its own language very similar to Spanish. Name it.

1019. Name the capital of the Armagnac region of France.

1020. Name the road linking Nice and Grenoble in France.

1011. Manhattan
1012. *Sake*
1013. *Lassi*
1014. Bolivia
1015. Baghdad
1016. Singhalese
1017. Josephine
1018. Gallego
1019. Condom
1020. Route Napoleon

QUESTIONS...

1021. On which Mediterranean island are the 5,000-year-old Ggatija temples located?

1022. The people of which Mediterranean islands speak a language derived from Arabic but written in the Roman script?

1023. Which American city did John Gunther call the "Athens of Dixie," and the "Protestant Vatican of the South"?

1024. The Metropolitan Museum is famous for its Egyptian collection. Where else can you see fine Egyptian artefacts in New York City?

1025. Frederick the Great of Prussia built 2 castles, Charlottenburg and Sans Souci. Which one is in Berlin?

1026. Which book would you turn to if you wanted to rate your travel achievements?

1027. One of the most important Zapotec sites can be seen at Monte Alban, Mexico. Which museum houses the art treasures found there?

1028. In which American state can you see the gigantic heads of Presidents Washington, Jefferson, Lincoln and Theodore Roosevelt carved on Mount Rushmore?

1029. The Rafael Larco Herrera Museum is known for its collection of nearly 55,000 erotic pottery figurines. Where can you visit it?

1030. These gigantic animals and birds traced on the desert sand are best seen from a plane. What country would you fly over?

1021. Gozo, Malta

1022. Malta, Gozo

1023. Nashville, Tennessee

1024. Brooklyn Museum

1025. Charlottenburg

1026. *Traveler's Challenge* by George Blagowidow (Hippocrene Books)

1027. Oaxaca Museum

1028. South Dakota

1029. Lima, Peru

1030. Peru

QUESTIONS...

1031. Which New York avenue is named after an American president, and is known as the home of the advertising and publishing industries?

1032. We know the Italian capital as "Rome"; what do its inhabitants call it?

1033. Vaduz, Valetta and Vienna are all European capitals beginning with "v". Name their countries.

1034. Most tourists come to Cuzco to visit which ancient Inca city?

1035. One of the highest-operating cablecars (built 1924-26) will carry you to the top of which mountain in Bavaria, Germany?

1036. The first Lutheran church in America was built by Russians. In which state?

1037. The Russian word for railroad station is *vokzal*. Which particular British station lent its name for this?

1038. "English soup" is a sumptuous dessert concocted of eggs, sugar and wine. Where could you eat it, and what would you ask for?

1039. "There is no greenery; it is enough to make a stone sad," said Nikita Krushchev; Le Corbusier called it "a beautiful catastrophe." Which American city is it?

1040. How many languages are spoken on the Iberian peninsula? Name them.

1031. Madison

1032. Roma

1033. Liechtenstein, Malta, Austria

1034. Machu Picchu

1035. Zugspitze

1036. Alaska

1037. Vauxhall, London

1038. Italy, *Zuppa Inglese*

1039. New York

1040. 5: Basque, Catalan, Galleno, Spanish, Portuguese

1041. Name the American cemetery where many military heros are buried.

1042. How many countries have territory north of the Arctic Circle? Name them.

1043. At the turn of the century, trams were the main form of urban mass transit. Name a U.S. city in which they operate today.

1044. Of what country are the Canary Islands a part?

1045. Which desert divides Israel and Egypt?

1046. In which Canadian province can you visit Dinosaur Park?

1047. Name a Central American country which shares its name with its largest city, but not with its capital.

1048. Which Atalntic island was the landing station of many U.S. immigrants?

1049. In the 19th century many German immigrants settled along a river which they called the "American Rhine". Name it.

1050. Canandaigua, Cayuga, Keuka, Oneida, Owasco, Seneca, and Skaneateles are all lakes in New York State. How are they known collectively?

...ANSWERS

1041. Arlington Cemetery

1042. 7: Canada, Denmark (Greenland), Findland, Norway, Sweden, U.S.A., U.S.S.R.

1043. San Francisco

1044. Spain

1045. Sinai

1046. Alberta

1047. Belize

1048. Ellis Island

1049. Ohio

1050. Finger Lakes

QUESTIONS...

1051. Where in Iran can you visit the ruins of King Darius' palace?

1052. The ziggurat of Ur is an enormous contsruction over 4,000 years old. In what country is it located today?

1053. Name the lake on which Chicago, Illinois stands.

1054. In how many North and Central American countries could you enjoy aquatic sports in both Atlantic and Pacific oceans?

1055. Name the fortress in which the Zealots made their final stand in 73 A.D.

1056. Many places are named for saints. In France the word is *Saint*, in Italy, *Santo*; what is the German equivalent?

1057. Which city houses the richest European museum of Jewish history?

1058. Mohenjo-Daro, where civilization flourished around 5,000 B.C. on the banks of the Indus River, is one of the most interesting archaeological sites of which country?

1059. In which country can you visit the Pohutu geyser and the Waitomo caves?

1060. In which town can you see the balcony where Romeo wooed Juliet?

1051. Perspolis

1052. Iraq

1053. Lake Michigan

1054. 6: Canada, Costa Rica, Mexico, Nicaragua, Panama, U.S.A.

1055. Masada

1056. *Sankt*

1057. Prague, Czechoslovakia

1058. Pakistan

1059. New Zealand

1060. Verona, Italy

QUESTIONS...

1061. Verdi's opera *Aida* takes place in which country?

1062. Lake Ontario is bordered on the north and west by Canada. Which American state lies to its south and east?

1063. St. Thomas, St. Kitts, San Andreas, St. Eustatius, St. Bartholomew and St. Lucia are all Caribbean islands named after saints. Which one is independent, and to what countries do each of the others belong?

1064. Name an island close to Spain famous for, amongst other things, its monkeys.

1065. Czechoslovakia's capital is known to us as "Prague". How is it spelled locally?

1066. A dependency of this country is 50.5 times bigger than it, but has only 1% of its population. Name the country and the dependency.

1067. Thingvellir, a plain of volcanic lava in Iceland, is also a historic site. Who used to meet there?

1068. Name the 6 African countries lying on the equator.

1069. Tennyson's poem *The Charge of the Light Brigade* celebrated a battle fought on what peninsula?

1070. The Allies' invasion of Europe in 1844 is commemorated by many monuments. In what French province did the soldiers first land?

...ANSWERS

1061. Egypt

1062. New York

1063. St. Lucia; U.S.A., Great Britain, Colombia, the Netherlands, France, respectively

1064. Gibraltar

1065. Praha

1066. Denmark, Greenland

1067. Ancient Icelandic parliament

1068. Congo, Gabon, Kenya, Somalia, Uganda, Zaire

1069. Crimea

1070. Normandy

1071. Name the country in which the Battle of the Bulge was fought in the winter of 1944/45.

1072. The U.S.A. entered World War II after a Japanese attack on an American harbor. Name it, and its state.

1073. Perugia, Orvieto and Assissi are medieval towns in which single Italian province?

1074. The Fragonnard Museum in Grasse, France is located in the artist's family home. A copy of *The Seasons*, one of his most important works, is on display there. Where can you see the original?

1075. Which Buddhist temple built about 2,000 years ago is well-preserved, and can be visited near the Indian city of Bhopal?

1076. What language, other than English, is spoken in Scotland?

1077. Nepal, the Netherlands and Norway have more in common than the letter "n". What is it?

1078. How are the Poles, the Lithuanians and the Hungarians different from the Romanians?

1079. The Serbian and Croatian languages are almost identical. Name their main difference.

1080. Traveling south from London along the prime meridian will take you to which African capital?

1071. Belgium

1072. Pearl Harbor, Hawaii

1073. Umbria

1074. Frick Museum, New York

1075. Sanchi

1076. Gaelic

1077. All are kingdoms

1078. They are Roman Catholics, while Romanians are Russian Orthodox Christians

1079. Serbian is written in Cyrillic characters, Croatian uses the Latin script

1080. Accra, Ghana

1081. Toronto is the capital of which Canadian province?

1082. On which African island is Magasay the language spoken?

1083. Which world-famous city can you visit in the Italian province of Lazio?

1084. A barren landscape known as the "Valley of the Moon" is located near which South American capital?

1085. What are LOT, LLOID and LASCA?

1086. Milan is the principal city of which Italian region?

1087. Arnheim, Cologne, Wiesbaden, Mainz, and Mannheim have a common denominator. Name it.

1088. Traveling less than 500 miles east from London would take you through which two European capitals?

1089. How many countries does the equator cross in the Americas? Name them.

1090. A famed museum of gold objects can be visited in Lima, Peru. Which other South American capital has a similar museum?

1081. Ontario

1082. Madagascar

1083. Rome

1084. La Paz, Bolivia

1085. National airlines of Poland, Bolivia, Costa Rica

1086. Lombardy

1087. River Rhine

1088. Brussels, Bonn

1089. 3: Brazil, Colombia, Ecuador

1090. Bogota, Colombia

QUESTIONS...

1091. In which South American capital can you visit a museum displaying about 30 varieties of potato?

1092. If you traveled along the international date line from the North Pole to Antarctica, how many countries would you pass through?

1093. Which is the only Asian country crossed by the equator?

1094. What language would you hear in the street when traveling through The Netherlands?

1095. Vilnius is the present capital of Lithuania. What was the capital between the world wars?

1096. What river flows in front of the U.S. Military Academy at West Point?

1097. What is the difference between the National Gallery in Washington, D.C., and New York's Metropolitan Museum: not in terms of art, but admissions policies?

1098. "A big hard-boiled city with no more personality than a paper cup," wrote Raymond Chandler of the American metropolis described by *Time* magazine as "the world's most celebrated suburb of nowhere." Where?

1099. Which Canadian province has the mildest climate?

1100. Name the feeling that you might experience after answering the last 1099 questions: the overwhelming desire to pack your bags and visit all these places.

1091. La Paz, Bolivia
1092. None
1093. Indonesia
1094. Dutch
1095. Kaunas
1096. Hudson
1097. The National Gallery is free
1098. Los Angeles
1099. British Colombia
1100. Dromomania

1101. What is the sequel to this book, in which you will find even more searching questions to titillate your wanderlust?

...ANSWERS

1101. *Traveler's I.Q. Test*